Warblers

OF EASTERN NORTH AMERICA

Warblers

OF EASTERN NORTH AMERICA

2ND EDITION

Chris G. Earley

FIREFLY BOOKS

A FIREFLY BOOK

Published by Firefly Books Ltd. 2023
Copyright © 2003, 2023 Chris Earley
Photographs © individual photographers, as credited

First Printing

Library of Congress Control Number: 2022946889

Library and Archives Canada Cataloguing in Publication
Title: Warblers of eastern North America / Chris G. Earley.
Other titles: Warblers of the Great Lakes Region and
     eastern North America
Names: Earley, Chris, 1968- author.
Description: 2nd edition. | Previous edition published under
     title: Warblers of the Great Lakes Region and eastern North
     America. | Includes bibliographical references and index.
Identifiers: Canadiana 20220435022 |
     ISBN 9780228104254 (softcover)
Subjects: LCSH: Wood warblers—Canada, Eastern—
     Identification. | LCSH: Wood warblers—East (U.S.)—
     Identification. | LCGFT: Field guides.
Classification: LCC QL696.P2438 E277 2023 |
     DDC 598.8/72097—dc23

Published in the U.S. by
Firefly Books (U.S.) Inc.
P.O. Box 1338, Ellicott Station
Buffalo, New York 14205

Published in Canada by
Firefly Books Ltd.
50 Staples Avenue, Unit 1
Richmond Hill, Ontario L4B 0A7

Design by Lind Design
Second edition revisions and cover design by Stacey Cho
Front cover photo © Brian E. Small
Back cover photo © Shutterstock/Paul Reeves Photography
Title page photo © Brian E. Small

Printed in China

FSC
www.fsc.org
MIX
Paper from
responsible sources
FSC® C160794

Canada [✦] We acknowledge the financial support
of the Government of Canada.

Table of Contents

Welcome to the world of warblers

THIS BOOK IS DESIGNED TO HELP YOU LEARN ABOUT the many warbler species that can be found in eastern North America. Because there are many different learning styles, this book presents warblers in a variety of ways. It is designed for both beginners and the experienced, covering the relatively easy spring males as well as the more difficult fall plumages.

Watching warblers in their environment reveals inter- actions that link all of nature together.

When trying to identify birds it is important to remember the following motto: *I don't know.*

Really, it's okay to say it! Too many birders will get an incon- clusive view of a bird and then just guess. With practice, you can identify birds from incredibly short glimpses of them, but there will always be some "I don't knows." And even if you do get a good look and still can't identify the warbler, you will have learned from the process. The next time you see that species, it will be familiar to you and you may see another field mark or behavior to help in its identification. And don't forget to watch the warblers as well! Keeping a checklist is fun and a way to record your sightings, but careful observations will help you really understand these interesting birds. Watching warblers in their environment reveals interactions that link all of nature together.

How to use this book

♂ MALE   **♀ FEMALE**

If there is no symbol, then the male/female plumage is not significantly different.

SPRING   Spring and summer months' plumage.

FALL   Autumn and winter months' plumage.

ADULT   Warblers that are over one year old (i.e., not in their first fall or first spring plumage).

FIRST FALL   Some warblers have a distinctive plumage during their first autumn and winter. In fall migration, these warblers are two to five months old.

FIRST SPRING   Some warblers have a distinctive plumage in their first full spring after they hatch. In spring migration, these warblers are almost one year old. Note that many males and females are slightly duller in their fall and/or first spring plumages.

LISTEN FOR   Learning and remembering warbler songs can be a rewarding and helpful undertaking. Most warbler species have two or more song types and variations. The ones given in this book are examples of what is commonly heard. Utilize another bird book for more examples as well as for learning their call notes (most warblers have distinctive non-song sounds that can be heard as they forage or scold potential predators). There are many great sound recordings, websites and phone apps that can help show the differences between species (see references on pages 112–113). Once you know a few of the songs you will be surprised at how many more warblers you'll see because you heard them first.

COMPARE TO   This lists other regularly seen warblers and even other bird groups (such as vireos or thrushes) that look similar to that particular warbler. A reference to the comparison pages (pages 120–131) may be listed here as well.

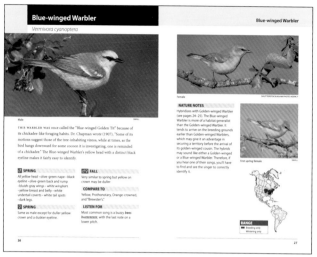

The color along the top of the page corresponds to the adult spring male's throat color. This is to help beginners find all spring males with that color throat for comparison purposes.

SEASONAL STATUS

This list (pages 14–15) refers to the seasonal status of warblers at Point Pelee National Park. Because Point Pelee is the central point for much of eastern North America, you can use this information as a guideline for when these birds may arrive or leave your area. For example, Point Pelee is at roughly the same latitude as Chicago and the northern border between Pennsylvania and New York state, so seasonal status in these areas may be similar. As another example, consider that the average spring first-arrival date of a migratory species at Point Pelee likely precedes the first-arrival date of that species in more northerly Milwaukee or Toronto by about two to six days.

RANGE MAPS

These maps show each species' breeding and wintering ranges.

A note to beginners

Watch the warbler for a while before flipping through this guide.

WHEN LOOKING AT warblers, resist the urge to instantly start flipping through this guide. Watch the bird first. This way you can look for field marks and behaviors before the bird disappears from your view. Ask yourself questions such as *What color is its throat? Does it have wingbars, an eyering, streaks on its breast, tail spots? Does it pump its tail? Is it singing?* If you have a notebook, write down your observations quickly and then use this book. Warblers move quickly through the foliage, and you should spend your time looking at them before they move on.

Try to learn the spring males first. They tend to be the easiest to observe because they do almost all of the singing, and thus attract attention to themselves with sound as well as sight. They also have the boldest markings and coloration, making identification a bit more straightforward. By learning the males really well, you will start to notice their patterns in the muted colors of the females. While watching the spring warblers, ask yourself questions such as *Does it have a long or short tail in relation to its body size? Does it move quickly or slowly? What shape is its bill?* Being familiar with the shape, size and movements of spring warblers will help with identification in the fall, when many warbler species are quite drab and similar.

The quotes

MANY OF THE warbler descriptions include a quote from earlier writings on warbler behavior and identification. While these observations may seem unscientific or "fluffy" to many readers, I believe that earlier naturalists had a magnificent understanding of warblers and their lives. While giving non-human creatures human characteristics (anthropomorphism) is unscientific, I believe that beginners can benefit from this practice. What better way for a human to initially learn about something than to use human-like descriptions? So try reading the quotes and then watch a warbler move through its habitat. You may find that the melodramatic or colorful style does indeed apply to your subject. If you still find the quotes aren't for you, just skip them and use the other information. There are many different learning styles.

While giving non-human creatures human characteristics is unscientific, beginners can benefit from this practice.

Taxonomy

THE WARBLERS COVERED in this book are all in the family *Parulidae,* or American Wood-warblers, a group of birds belonging to North, Central and South America. The name "warbler" also refers to a similar-looking but unrelated group of birds from the Old World. The order of the warblers in this book follows the seventh edition of the *American Ornithologists' Union Check-list of North American Birds*, 1998, and its supplements.

The name "warbler" also refers to a similar-looking but unrelated group of birds from the Old World.

The warblers are arranged in a specific sequence (taxonomic order) that recognizes relationships between species. You will notice that many closely related warblers will have similar behaviors, shapes and beak sizes, even though their markings might be quite different. This order may help you to use shape and behavior as identification aids as well as learn a bit about taxonomic relationships among birds.

Warbler look-alikes

Philadelphia
Vireo

NOT ONLY CAN identifying the different warblers be confusing at first, just figuring out if what you are looking at is indeed a warbler can be the initial challenge. One group of birds that is very similar to these warblers is the vireos. Vireos tend to be slightly bigger and chunkier than warblers and have a heavier bill that is tipped with a small hook.

Tennessee
Warbler

The Ruby-crowned Kinglet and Golden-crowned Kinglet look like warblers as well, but they are smaller than warblers and their heads look quite large in relation to their body size. The Empidonax flycatchers, such as the Least Flycatcher, are also similar to many warblers because of their size and the presence of wingbars and eyerings. When looking for warblers, you will undoubtedly come across their look-alikes, so take some time to observe the look-alikes' foraging techniques and listen to their calls and songs.

SHUTTERSTOCK/2009FOTOFRIENDS

Ruby-crowned Kinglet

Least Flycatcher   SHUTTERSTOCK/AGAMI PHOTO AGENCY

Warbling Vireo   SHUTTERSTOCK/AGAMI PHOTO AGENCY

Identification features

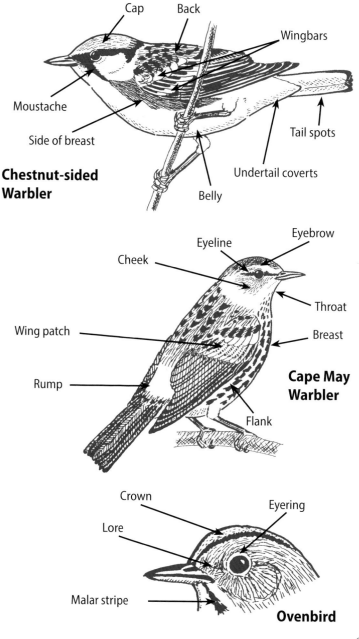

Cap
Back
Wingbars
Moustache
Side of breast
Chestnut-sided Warbler
Belly
Undertail coverts
Tail spots

Eyeline
Eyebrow
Cheek
Throat
Wing patch
Breast
Rump
Cape May Warbler
Flank

Crown
Eyering
Lore
Malar stripe
Ovenbird

CHRIS EARLEY

Seasonal status of warblers
for Point Pelee National Park

Month	J	F	M	A	M	J	J	A	S	O	N	D
☐ Ovenbird												
☐ Worm-eating Warbler												
☐ Louisiana Waterthrush												
☐ Northern Waterthrush												
☐ Golden-winged Warbler												
☐ Blue-winged Warbler												
☐ Black-and-white Warbler												
☐ Prothonotary Warbler												
☐ Swainson's Warbler												
☐ Tennessee Warbler												
☐ Orange-crowned Warbler												
☐ Nashville Warbler												
☐ Virginia's Warbler												
☐ Connecticut Warbler												
☐ Mourning Warbler												
☐ Kentucky Warbler												
☐ Common Yellowthroat												
☐ Hooded Warbler												
☐ American Redstart												
☐ Kirtland's Warbler												
☐ Cape May Warbler												

FROM J.R. GRAHAM, 1996

Common   **Uncommon**   —— **Rare**   ----- **Very Rare**

Month	J	F	M	A	M	J	J	A	S	O	N	D
☐ Cerulean Warbler												
☐ Northern Parula												
☐ Magnolia Warbler												
☐ Bay-breasted Warbler												
☐ Blackburnian Warbler												
☐ Yellow Warbler												
☐ Chestnut-sided Warbler												
☐ Blackpoll Warbler												
☐ Black-throated Blue Warbler												
☐ Palm Warbler												
☐ Pine Warbler												
☐ Yellow-rumped Warbler												
☐ Yellow-throated Warbler												
☐ Prairie Warbler												
☐ Grace's Warbler												
☐ Black-throated Gray Warbler												
☐ Townsend's Warbler												
☐ Hermit Warbler												
☐ Black-throated Green Warbler												
☐ Canada Warbler												
☐ Wilson's Warbler												

Seiurus aurocapilla

AN EASIER BIRD to hear than to see, the Ovenbird is very thrush-like in its appearance and the way it stays on the forest floor, earning it the earlier name of "Golden-crowned Thrush." The name "Ovenbird" comes from the fact that its nest is domed, with a side entrance, similar to an old-fashioned oven. When leaving its nest it is very cautious, as noted by Wilson (in Studer, 1881): "When alarmed, it escapes from the nest in great silence and rapidity running along the ground like a worm, as if afraid to tread too heavily on the leaves."

ALL PLUMAGES

Two black stripes on either side of an orange crown (Latin name *aurocapillus* means gold-hair) • *whitish eyering • white throat* • black moustache • brownish-olive back and rump • white underparts • *dark spots on breast and sides* • pinkish legs • no tail spots.

COMPARE TO

Northern Waterthrush and Louisiana Waterthrush, Wood Thrush and Swainson's Thrush.

LISTEN FOR

Loud series of **teacher, teacher, teacher, teacher**, that gets louder towards the end.

Walking on the forest floor

NATURE NOTES

Along with the White-throated Sparrow, the Ovenbird is the most abundant species to collide with lit buildings in Toronto during night migration. The organization FLAP (Fatal Light Awareness Program) works to prevent nighttime migrants such as warblers from flying into city buildings (see page 110 for more details). As with many other warbler species, fall migration occurs during a much longer time frame than in the spring. In Michigan, some Ovenbirds begin to migrate south in mid-July, while others move through as late as early October. In 1929, Robert Frost wrote a poem about the Ovenbird: "There is a singer everyone has heard, /Loud, a mid-summer and a mid-wood bird…."

Note orange crown stripe

RANGE
■ Breeding only
  Wintering only

Helmitheros vermivorum

THIS DISTINCTIVE-LOOKING warbler can be a challenging one to see. Brewster (1875) wrote that the Worm-eating Warbler "vanishes unaccountably before your eyes, leaving you quite uncertain where to look for it next; indeed, I hardly know a more difficult bird to procure, for the slightest noise sends it darting off through the woods at once." Audubon (in Studer, 1881) seems to have had a bit more luck, at least in watching this species, "as they are seen continually moving about, nestling among the leaves, and scarcely ever removing from one situation to another, until after they have made a full inspection of the part in which they have been employed."

SHUTTERSTOCK/JUKKA JANTUNEN

ALL PLUMAGES

Buffy head · dark eyeline · *dark stripes on sides of crown* · olive-green upperparts · *buffy underparts* · no tail spots · pinkish legs.

LISTEN FOR

A dry Chipping Sparrow-like trill.

NATURE NOTES

Many animals have been recorded as possible nest predators of this ground-nesting warbler. One female obviously knew her nest was vulnerable; she was seen to cover the nest with a leaf when she left to find food! The name "Worm-eating" actually refers to the caterpillars or insect larva that all warblers eat, not earthworms. This warbler often feeds on insects found in clusters of dead leaves. It is estimated that over 2000 migrating Worm-eating Warblers died while crossing the Gulf of Mexico in a severe storm near Louisiana in April 1995.

RANGE

■ Breeding only
　 Wintering only

Parkesia motacilla

WHILE STUDER MAY have liked the song of the Northern Waterthrush (see pages 22–23), Audubon (in Studer, 1881) preferred that of the Louisiana Waterthrush: "As much and justly as the song of the Nightingale is admired, I am inclined, after having listened to it, to pronounce it in no degree superior to that of the Louisiana Waterthrush." Where their ranges overlap in the Great Lakes region, the Louisiana Waterthrush prefers fast-moving water such as streams and small rivers, whereas the Northern Waterthrush usually inhabits the standing water areas of swamps, bogs and the shores of lakes.

ALL PLUMAGES

White eyebrow (possibly gray or buffy near the eye) that does not get thinner behind the eye • brown eyeline • brown upperparts • white underparts with dark streaks • often some buff on flanks • *usually bright pink legs.*

COMPARE TO

Northern Waterthrush (see comparison pages 120–121), Ovenbird, Gray-cheeked Thrush, Hermit Thrush, Swainson's Thrush and Wood Thrush.

LISTEN FOR

A song that starts off with a few loud whistles, then changes to a scrambled mix of quieter twittering notes.

REAUME

NATURE NOTES

Even though the Louisiana Waterthrush looks extremely similar to the Northern Waterthrush, there are no records of them ever hybridizing.

SHUTTERSTOCK/RAY HENNESSY

RANGE
■ Breeding only
Wintering only

Parkesia noveboracensis

REAUME

BOTH SPECIES OF waterthrush may remind you of a Spotted Sandpiper teetering its rear end as it forages along the edge of a wet area. This warbler can be quite shy and hard to see. Its timidity was noted by Studer (1881): "It is very shy and darts out of sight at the most careful approach. When tired of feeding, it will perch on some favorite branch overhanging the water, and pour forth a song at once sweet, expressive and charming. This song always commences with loud, clear, and vivacious notes, falling in almost imperceptible gradations until they are scarcely articulated."

ALL PLUMAGES

Light yellow, buffy or white eyebrow that usually gets thinner behind the eye • brown eyeline • brown upperparts • *light yellow, buffy or white underparts* with dark streaks • often dark spots on throat • dull pink legs.

COMPARE TO

Louisiana Waterthrush (see comparison pages 120–121), Ovenbird, Gray-cheeked Thrush, Hermit Thrush, Swainson's Thrush and Wood Thrush.

LISTEN FOR

A loud series of fluid notes *weet weet weet weet wee wee wee chew chew chew*.

Walking on the forest floor

SHUTTERSTOCK/MATTHEW JOLLEY

NATURE NOTES

Once called the Short-billed Waterthrush, as its beak is usually shorter than that of the Louisiana Waterthrush. Northern Waterthrushes often nest in the tangled root systems of fallen trees. They will sometimes eat small minnows.

REAUME

RANGE
- Breeding only
- Wintering only

Golden-winged Warbler

Vermivora chrysoptera

Male

SMALL

THE GOLDEN-WINGED WARBLER is a striking warbler, and also one of the easiest to identify. Winsor Marrett Tyler wrote, "The golden-winged warbler is one of the daintiest among this group of gay-colored little birds. Its plumage is immaculate white below and delicate pearl-gray on the upperparts, the crown and wings sparkle with golden yellow, and on the throat and cheeks is a broad splash of jet black" (in Bent, 1953). This warbler's golden wing patches (its Latin name, *chrysoptera,* means "gold-wing") and bold facial pattern help beginners identify it without too much trouble.

♂ SPRING

Black throat and cheeks • white moustache • *yellow crown* • white eyebrow • gray back and rump • *golden-yellow wing patch* • whitish breast, belly and undertail coverts • white tail spots • dark legs.

♀ SPRING

Same as male except for • *gray throat* • *gray cheeks* • greenish-yellow crown • two golden-yellow wingbars.

♂♀ FALL

Very similar to spring but may have some greenish feathers on crown and nape.

24

Female

LISTEN FOR

Most common song is a buzzy **bees buzz buzz buzz** with the first note higher than the similarly pitched buzz notes.

NATURE NOTES

The Golden-winged Warbler's breeding range has been changing for over 100 years and still seems to be. While it becomes scarcer in the southeast portions of its range, it becomes more abundant to the northwest. Hybridization and competition with the Blue-winged Warbler, as well as nest parasitism by Brown-headed Cowbirds, may be the cause of localized declines of the Golden-winged Warbler. In Ontario, the first breeding record was near London in 1912, and by 1948 it was breeding near Toronto. It now nests as far north as Sault Ste. Marie and North Bay, and its numbers have declined in its former southern Ontario range. Because of its white underparts and black throat, the male may at first appear to be a Black-capped Chickadee, a species that Golden-winged Warblers may be seen with during their stay in North America.

From underneath, this warbler looks like a chickadee

SMALL

RANGE
 Breeding only
Wintering only

Blue-winged Warbler

Vermivora cyanoptera

Male

SMALL

THIS WARBLER WAS once called the "Blue-winged Golden Tit" because of its chickadee-like foraging habits. Dr. Chapman wrote (1907), "Some of its motions suggest those of the tree-inhabiting vireos, while at times, as the bird hangs downward for some cocoon it is investigating, one is reminded of a chickadee." The Blue-winged Warbler's yellow head with a distinct black eyeline makes it fairly easy to identify.

♂ SPRING

All yellow head • olive-green nape • *black eyeline* • olive-green back and rump • bluish-gray wings • *white wingbars* • yellow breast and belly • white undertail coverts • white tail spots • dark legs.

♀ SPRING

Same as male except for duller yellow crown and a duskier eyeline.

♂♀ FALL

Very similar to spring but yellow on crown may be duller.

COMPARE TO

Yellow, Prothonotary, Orange-crowned, and "Brewster's."

LISTEN FOR

Most common song is a buzzy *bees buzzzzzzzzz*, with the last note on a lower pitch.

Female

SHUTTERSTOCK/AGAMI PHOTO AGENCY

NATURE NOTES

Hybridizes with Golden-winged Warbler (see pages 24–25). The Blue-winged Warbler is more of a habitat generalist than the Golden-winged Warbler. It tends to arrive on the breeding grounds earlier than Golden-winged Warblers, which may give it an advantage in securing a territory before the arrival of its golden-winged cousin. The hybrids may sound like either a Golden-winged or a Blue-winged Warbler. Therefore, if you hear one of their songs, you'll have to find and see the singer to correctly identify it.

First spring female

SMALL

RANGE

■ Breeding only
  Wintering only

Vermivora cyanoptera x Vermivora chrysoptera

Male "Lawrence's" SHUTTERSTOCK/RAY HENNESSY

Male "Lawrence's" SHUTTERSTOCK/JAY ONDREICKA

THE BLUE-WINGED Warbler and the Golden-winged Warbler frequently hybridize where their ranges overlap. The resulting offspring were once thought to be separate species: the "Brewster's" Warbler and the rarer "Lawrence's" Warbler. Quotes are now put around the names to show that they are not truly separate species.

The genetics that control what Blue-winged Warbler x Golden-winged Warbler hybrids look like are not as straightforward as was once thought. The amount of yellow in a hybrid's plumage, for example, depends on many variables. To make things more confusing, some individuals can even become less yellow as they grow older.

The presence of a throat patch, however, seems to be a little more straightforward. A black or gray throat patch and mask appears to be a recessive trait and so is rarer than not having a throat patch and mask.

For birding purposes, the individuals with these throat patches are usually considered "Lawrence's" Warblers while the hybrids with an eyeline but no throat patch are the more commonly seen "Brewster's" Warblers.

All of the hybrids and the Golden-winged and Blue-winged Warblers can interbreed, and pure-looking Golden-winged and Blue-winged Warblers often carry genes from the other's gene pool. Luckily, none of these details stop us from enjoying the thrill of seeing a hybrid and marveling at its unique color pattern!

Male "Brewster's" SMALL

Male "Brewster's" McCAW

Male "Brewster's" SHUTTERSTOCK/FOTOREQUEST

A dull female "Lawrence's" SMALL

A very yellowish female "Brewster's"

SHUTTERSTOCK/AGAMI PHOTO AGENCY

Mniotilta varia

Spring male

THE BLACK-AND-WHITE Warbler is the only warbler that regularly forages by creeping along the trunks of trees, earning it names such as "Pied Creeper" and "Black-and-white Nuthatch." Of this "Black-and-white Creeper," Studer (1881) wrote, "He seldom perches on small twigs, but circumambulates the trunk and larger branches, in quest of ants and other insects, with admirable dexterity. He is evidently nearer related to the Creepers than to the Warblers."

♂ SPRING

Black and white striped overall • white eyebrow, moustache and stripe on crown • black stripe on sides of crown • *black cheek and throat* • white wingbars • black and white striped back • black rump • white underparts • black streaks on breast, belly and undertail coverts • large white spots in tail • dark legs. (First spring male has less or no black in throat.)

♀ SPRING

Similar to spring adult male but has • *white throat* • *light gray cheeks* • thick black eyeline extending behind eye • may have buffy flanks • less distinct streaking on underparts.

♂ FALL

Similar to spring but usually has a whitish throat with black spots. (First fall male like spring female but with no buff in flanks.)

Spring female

REAUME

♀ FALL

Slightly buffier underparts than in spring. (First fall females may have more buff underneath than adult fall females.)

COMPARE TO

Blackpoll Warbler.

LISTEN FOR

A high-pitched *weesy weesy weesy weesy*.

NATURE NOTES

When foraging, Black-and-white Warblers, like nuthatches, do not use their tails as props like woodpeckers and Brown Creepers. A leg-banded Black-and-white Warbler was known to be at least eleven years and three months old – one of the oldest warblers on record.

Spring female showing off

SMALL

RANGE

■ Breeding only
  Wintering only

Prothonotary Warbler

Protonotaria citrea

Spring male

SHUTTERSTOCK/AGAMI PHOTO AGENCY

THE GOLDEN COLOR of this warbler gave it the name "Prothonotary," which refers to special religious scribes who wore yellow hoods. Chapman (1907) wrote, "This glowing bit of birdlife gleamed like a torch in the night…. His golden plumes were displayed as though for my special benefit."

♂ SPRING

All yellow head • green back • gray rump • *yellow breast and belly* • white undertail coverts • *bluish-gray wings* • dark legs • white spots in tail.

♀ SPRING

Slightly duller overall with a greenish-yellow crown and nape.

FALL

Similar to spring but with a bit more greenish-yellow in crown and nape.

COMPARE TO

Blue-winged, Yellow, Hooded, Wilson's.

LISTEN FOR

Loud, clear series of notes **weet weet weet weet weet**.

NATURE NOTES

The Prothonotary Warbler is eastern North America's only cavity-nesting warbler. It frequently competes with House Wrens for nest sites, which include human-made nest boxes (see pages 110–111). As the female builds the real nest, the male builds "dummy" nests in other cavities, possibly to fool predators. House Wrens may destroy this warbler's eggs when competing for nest sites.

Spring male

McCAW

Spring female

McCAW

Likely a first spring male but possibly a bright
spring female

REAUME

RANGE

- Breeding only
- Wintering only

Limnothlypis swainsonii

SMALL

A SECRETIVE WARBLER that occupies a variety of densely vegetated habitats in the southeastern United States, the drably colored Swainson's Warbler is much more likely to be heard than seen. The male sings a loud, rich song that gives away his presence, but it will still require patience to actually see him. The Swainson's Warbler often forages on the ground and moves about with a jerky hop-walk that it may use to scare its insect prey out into the open. It will also lift or flip over fallen leaves to look for hidden insects and other invertebrates.

ALL PLUMAGES

Dull rufous cap • light eyebrow • dark eyeline • long beak for a warbler • olive-brown upperparts • dull white, buffy or slightly yellowish throat, breast and belly • often whiter undertail coverts • no tail spots • pinkish legs.

COMPARE TO

Worm-eating, female Black-throated Blue, Tennessee, Carolina Wren.

LISTEN FOR

The clear song starts with high, thin whistles and changes to richer dropping notes.

SMALL

NATURE NOTES

Male Swainson's Warblers have been known to guard their mates from neighboring males prior to egg-laying. Female Swainson's Warblers may move along the ground acting like they have a broken wing to lure potential predators away from their nests.

SMALL

RANGE

Breeding only
Wintering only

Leiothlypis peregrina

Male

WHEN IT WAS FIRST discovered during migration in Tennessee, this warbler was considered rare and was thought to have strayed from its normal range (the name *peregrina* means "wanderer"). Alexander Skutch, an ornithologist in Central America, thought this warbler would be better named "Coffee Warbler," because it spends so much time in coffee plantations in its wintering grounds.

♂ SPRING

Gray head • white eyebrow and throat • dark eyeline • bright green back and rump • whitish underparts (sometimes a light yellow wash on breast) • may have white spots in tail • dark legs.

♀ SPRING

Similar to male except for • grayish-green head • *yellowish eyebrow and throat* • light yellow on breast and sides • often no white spots in tail • closely resembles both the Warbling and the Philadelphia Vireo (see page 12).

♂ FALL ADULT

Similar to spring male except • grayish green head • throat may be light yellow instead of white • back is duller than spring but may still have some bright green feathers • some light yellow on breast usually present • *white undertail coverts*.

Female — SHUTTERSTOCK/AGAMI PHOTO AGENCY

Fall — McCAW

♀ FALL   ♂ FIRST FALL

Similar to spring female except olive-green head • dusky eyeline • may have indistinct wing bars • more yellow on breasts and sides. (Some individuals may have a yellowish tinge to belly and undertail coverts.)

COMPARE TO

Spring females and fall birds may be confused with the Pine, Orange-crowned, female Cerulean, female Yellow Warbler, Philadelphia Vireo, and Warbling Vireo.

LISTEN FOR

Usually a three-parted song of staccato notes, the last part being the fastest. *Picka picka picka picka, seat seat, sit-sit-sit-sit-sit-sit-sit*.

NATURE NOTES

It has been estimated that some areas may have up to 610 pairs/km² of this species during spruce budworm outbreaks in Ontario's boreal forests.

Fall — FAIRBAIRN

RANGE
■ Breeding only
  Wintering only

Leiothlypis celata

Spring

SMALL

IRENE G. WHEELOCK wrote of the Orange-crowned Warbler, "All day long he flits about through the oak trees, leaning away over the tips of the boughs to investigate a spray of leaves, or stretching up his pretty head to reach a blossom just above him; now clinging head downward underneath a spray, or hovering under the yellow tassels as a bee hovers beneath a flower" (in Bent, 1953). Her description beautifully describes the feeding habits of this and other *Leiothlypis* warblers. Though they will hover to gain access to insects if they can't reach them from a twig, they usually stretch or hang to glean their prey from leaves, blossoms and the ends of branches. It is only because of these acrobatic movements that you may be able to see how the Orange-crowned Warbler got its name. The dull orange crown is not only hard to see, it is often concealed (its Latin name, *celata*, means "concealed") and may even be absent in some females. Fall migration can be an especially confusing time to try to identify these warblers.

Showing orange crown and breast streaks

Note the yellow undertail coverts

SHUTTERSTOCK/WINGMAN PHOTOGRAPHY

SPRING

*Short dusky eyeline • pale indistinct
eyebrow • faint narrow broken eyering*
• orange crown (may be concealed or
absent) • dull whitish-olive throat • olive-
green back, a bit brighter at the rump
• yellowish-olive underparts with brighter
yellow undertail coverts • faint streaks on
sides of breast • no tail spots • dark legs.

FALL

Similar to spring birds, but a bit grayer
overall, especially on the heads of some.

Fall

SHUTTERSTOCK/PAUL REEVES PHOTOGRAPHY

COMPARE TO

Spring female or fall Tennessee, dull
female Yellow, female Wilson's, Nashville,
Mourning, female Black-throated Blue. (See
Fall Comparison Chart 1, pages 122–123.)

LISTEN FOR

A weak trill that may drop in pitch.

NATURE NOTES

Will feed at sapsucker sap wells.
Orange-crowned Warblers have lice that
breed at the same time as their warbler
hosts. This helps the lice spread to the
nestlings before they leave the nest.

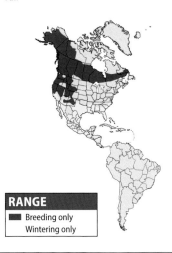

RANGE
■ Breeding only
  Wintering only

Leiothlypis ruficapilla

Male

SMALL

THIS BUSY WARBLER is often easily seen as it forages low in trees and shrubs. Chapman (1907) wrote that, during migration, "it is not particularly shy and often seems quite unconscious of the presence of the observer … giving us a glimpse of green and gold among the blossoms and opening leaves." Alexander Wilson discovered this warbler during migration near Nashville, Tennessee, in 1811.

♂ SPRING

Bluish-gray head • yellow throat • white eyering • chestnut patch on crown • olive-green back • greenish-yellow rump • yellow breast • whitish belly • yellow undertail coverts • no tail spots • dark legs.

♀ SPRING

Similar to the spring male but with a brownish-gray head • little chestnut on crown • yellow underneath is duller (first spring female is even duller).

♂♀ FALL

Similar to spring but duller overall. (First fall female can be very dull and even have a whitish throat and more white in the belly area • Still has an eyering.)

Female

SMALL

SHUTTERSTOCK/PAUL REEVES PHOTOGRAPHY

Singing male showing yellow-white-yellow underparts – a quite distinctive field mark when you can get a good look

RANGE

- ◾ Breeding only
- ◽ Wintering only

Nashville Warbler

Fall

Wet birds may appear to have breast streaks

EARLEY

COMPARE TO

Connecticut, Mourning, Orange-crowned and Common Yellowthroat.

LISTEN FOR

It has a two-parted song with the second part being a lower, dry trill *seat-it seat-it seat-it seat-it sitsitsitsitsitsit*.

NATURE NOTES

Before the mid-1800s the Nashville Warbler was considered to be rare. But because this warbler favors a wide variety of second-growth habitats, it has benefited from the initial clearing of land as well as from current clear-cutting practices. During fall migration in the eastern part of North America, adults tend to migrate inland, but first fall birds tend to migrate along the east coast. The Tennessee Warbler's song is quite similar to the Nashville Warbler's. To remember which has what song, note that the Nashville has a two-syllable name and a two-part song and the Tennessee has a three-syllable name and usually a three-part song.

First spring female

Spring male showing rufus feathers in cap

Oporornis agilis

SMALL

Spring male

THE CONNECTICUT WARBLER'S species name, *agilis*, describes its active ability to conceal itself from the observer. When you do actually get one in sight through your binoculars, you'll be amazed at how the bird seems to glide along the forest floor as it walks with careful steps. The walking is a good field identification feature, as most other warblers hop (exceptions being the Ovenbird, Kentucky Warbler and the waterthrushes). When singing, it can sit very still and seems to throw its voice, making it difficult to pinpoint. The name "Connecticut" refers to where the bird was found during migration by Alexander Wilson in 1812.

♂ SPRING

Bluish-gray hood covering the head • *bold white eyering* • olive-green upperparts • *yellow underparts* with some olive-green on sides • pink legs • no tail spots.

♀ SPRING

Similar to male except for a brownish hood and buffy or whitish throat.

♂♀ FALL

Birds similar but a bit duller than spring birds, eyering may be broken behind the eye. (First fall birds similar to fall adult female.)

Fall   TOMLINSON

SIMILAR SPECIES

Mourning, Yellowthroat, Nashville.

LISTEN FOR

A loud *chuckity-chuckity-chuckity-chuck*, somewhat similar to the Common Yellowthroat's song.

NATURE NOTES

This warbler has different spring and fall migration routes. In the spring it travels northwards inland, while in fall it heads to the East Coast and then travels south by doing a non-stop flight over the Atlantic Ocean to the southern Caribbean islands or northern South America.

Spring male   SMALL

RANGE
- Breeding only
- Wintering only

45

Geothlypis philadelphia

Spring male

ALEXANDER WILSON NAMED this warbler "Mourning" because of the black markings on the male's breast. Disagreeing with Wilson, Forbush (1929) wrote that "the marking about the breast is the only thing about the bird that would suggest mourning, for it seems as happy and active as most birds, and its song is a paean of joy." The Mourning Warbler moves about quickly in underbrush and low thickets and can be hard to see.

♂ SPRING

Bluish-gray hood • may have dusky lores • *variable dark patch on breast* • a few may have a very thin, white broken eyering • olive upperparts • *yellow underparts* • pinkish legs • no tail spots.

♀ SPRING

Is similar to the male except for having a • *light gray hood* • no black on breast • *throat may be buffy or whitish* • may have a thin broken eyering.

♀ FALL   ♂ FIRST FALL

Similar to spring adult female except for • head and upperparts all olive or brownish with yellowish or whitish throat (fall adult female with a more grayish hood) • thin whitish broken eyering or possibly a complete eyering. (First fall males may have some black spots on breast.)

COMPARE TO

Connecticut, Common Yellowthroat.

Spring female McCAW

Spring male REAUME

LISTEN FOR

A loud *cheery cheery cheery chorry chorry*, with the chorry notes lower in pitch than the cheery notes.

NATURE NOTES

The Mourning Warbler's preferred breeding habitat is second-growth clearings and disturbed woods, so it has likely benefited from logging practices.

Very dull first spring male showing a thin broken eyering and whitish throat

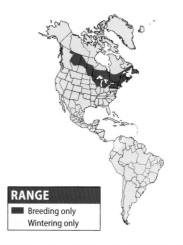

RANGE

- Breeding only
- Wintering only

Geothlypis formosa

Spring male

AS THE KENTUCKY WARBLER spends much of its time on the ground in very dense greenery, you may have to wait for it to jump onto a fallen log or bare branch to see its "Elvis" sideburns. Studer's (1881) observations of this warbler accurately describe its behavior: "It is a beautiful bird, very lively and sprightly in its habits, frequenting low, damp places in the wood. Very rarely is it found indulging in any elevated flight, but moving rapidly along dim forest paths, peering under leaves for some unfortunate spider or bug, occasionally leaping a few inches into the air to catch some dainty morsel screened in hanging leaves."

♂ SPRING

Black crown with grayish blue flecks towards nape • *yellow eyebrow joined to an eye-crescent behind eye* • black lores joined to *black "sideburns"* • *yellow throat* • olive-green upperparts • *yellow underparts* • pink legs • no tail spots.

♀ SPRING

Similar to male but usually has *less defined black* on head.

FALL

Similar to spring but with less defined black on head. (First fall females only show some dusky coloration where the black on the head is in adults.)

Spring female

SHUTTERSTOCK/AGAMI PHOTO AGENCY

COMPARE TO

Hooded, Canada, Mourning, Common Yellowthroat.

LISTEN FOR

A loud, clear series of notes such as *cheery cheery cheery cheery*.

NATURE NOTES

In its winter range, this warbler may follow army ants and feed on insects that the ants scare into view.

Likely a first spring female

SHUTTERSTOCK/AGAMI PHOTO AGENCY

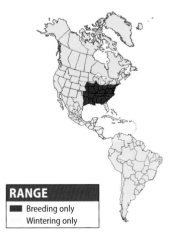

RANGE	
■	Breeding only
	Wintering only

Spring male

McCAW

MAKING IT LOOK like the Lone Ranger of the warbler world, the male Common Yellowthroat's black mask is a distinctive field mark. Its older name of "Olive-colored Yellow-throated Wren" describes the Yellowthroat's coloring and its wren-like jerky movements with tail cocked upwards. Chapman (1907) writes, "With nervous animation the bird hops here and there, appearing and disappearing, its bright eyes shining through its black mask, its personality so distinct, that one is tempted to believe it is a feather-clad sprite of the bushes."

♂ SPRING

Black mask on face bordered with dull white • yellow throat and breast • whitish or buffy belly • yellow undertail coverts • dull olive upperparts • no tail spots • dark to light brown legs.

♀ SPRING

Similar but with • no (or very little) black or white on face • suggestion of a light eyebrow and eyering.

♀ FALL   ♂ FALL ADULT

Similar to spring adults but with browner flanks. (First fall females similar to fall adult females but with less yellow and more buff on underparts.)

♂ FIRST FALL

Appears to have dirty cheeks with black suggesting a mask.

Spring female SHUTTERSTOCK/MATTHEW JOLLEY

Fall female SHUTTERSTOCK/CHRISTOPHER UNSWORTH

COMPARE TO

Females to Mourning, Kentucky, Connecticut, Nashville, Wilson's.

LISTEN FOR

A clear *witchity-witchity-witchity-witch*.

NATURE NOTES

This warbler is a common bird of wet areas, where its song can be heard emanating from the cattails or thickets. With the Song Sparrow and the Yellow Warbler, this is one of the three most frequent hosts of the Brown-headed Cowbird. The Common Yellowthroat may be the most abundant warbler in North America.

First fall female SHUTTERSTOCK/MELINDA FAWVER

First fall male SHUTTERSTOCK/BRIAN E KUSHNER

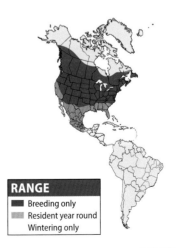

RANGE
■ Breeding only
▨ Resident year round
Wintering only

51

Hooded Warbler

Setophaga citrina

Spring male

FAIRBAIRN

THE MALE HOODED Warbler is a beautiful bird that is always met with smiles from birders. In 1907 Frank Chapman wrote, "Its beauty of plumage, charm of voice, and gentleness of demeanor, make it indeed not only a lovely, but a truly lovable bird." It often flashes the white in its tail, which could be a technique used to startle prey into the open (as hypothesized for the American Redstart).

♂ SPRING

Black hood covering throat, crown, nape • yellow forehead and cheeks • dusky lores • olive-green back and rump • yellow underparts (Latin name citrina means "lemon-colored") • pinkish legs • white tail spots.

♀ SPRING

As for the male except for • variable amounts of black "hood," from traces that only border cheeks to almost as much as the male, but usually has some yellow on the chin and greenish feathers in the nape • dusky lores. (First fall female and first spring female usually have no black or only traces of black on head.)

COMPARE TO

Female Wilson's and female Yellow.

LISTEN FOR

A series of whistles, described by Chapman (1907) as ***come to the woods or you won't see me***. Also described as ***weety weety weety-o***, similar to the Magnolia Warbler but with richer whistles.

Spring female

NATURE NOTES

In Connecticut, Hooded Warblers have been found to carry ticks infected with Lyme disease. Males and females use different habitats on wintering grounds – males use mature forest and females use scrub, secondary forest and disturbed areas. These warblers nest from May to August; having late nests reduces the chances of nest parasitism by Brown-headed Cowbirds. One predator in its wintering grounds is the Neotropical Green Frog.

Spring male showing tail spots

First spring female

RANGE
■ Breeding only
□ Wintering only

American Redstart

Setophaga ruticilla

Spring adult male

REAUME

I REFER TO two of our warblers as "Halloween Warblers." The male American Redstart is the only warbler besides the Blackburnian that combines orange, black and white in its adult male plumage. The American Redstart's behavior is so flycatcher-like that Studer wrote in 1881, "…we would rather have him placed among the *Muscicapidae* (flycatcher family)…the formation of his bill, the forward-pointing bristles, and especially his manners, stamp him a Flycatcher." This warbler's scientific name actually means "red-tailed moth-eater." The American Redstart is also distinctive when foraging or defending its territory, as it often flashes its wings and tail, revealing brightly colored patches of orange or yellow.

♂ SPRING ADULT

All black head and black back • black rump • *orange patches* at the base of the wing flight feathers, outer tail feathers, and the sides of breast • black breast • white belly and undertail coverts • dark legs.

♀ ADULT   ♂ FIRST FALL

Gray head • a thin, broken whitish eyering • whitish throat • olive back and rump • *yellowish patches* where it is orange on the adult male – wing patches are variable in size (first fall female may have no yellow in wing) • white underparts with yellow or

Spring female

REAUME

yellow-orange patches on the sides of breast.

♂ FIRST SPRING

Similar to adult female except for • dark lores • may have black markings on throat, breast and uppertail coverts (the area where the rump meets the tail feathers).

LISTEN FOR

A variable series of high notes that may end with an accented downslurred note.

NATURE NOTES

The American Redstart has prominent rictal bristles around its mouth and a broad-based bill, just like many flycatchers. These adaptations help these birds catch flying insects. This warbler is often attacked by Least Flycatchers because the two species compete for a similar food source. The flashing of its wings and tail while foraging may be a hunting technique used to startle insects and spiders out into the open. Its name comes from its resemblance to the unrelated European Redstart, "steort" meaning tail. (Yes, I agree that "American Orangestart" might be more appropriate!)

RANGE
■ Breeding only
  Wintering only

Spring female (likely her first spring)

Spring adult male with tail spread

Singing spring adult male showing rictal bristles around beak

Spring female

SHUTTERSTOCK/AGAMI PHOTO AGENCY

First spring male

REAUME

Kirtland's Warbler

Setophaga kirtlandii

Spring male

IF THE BACHMAN'S WARBLER is truly extinct (which is likely), the Kirtland's Warbler is North America's rarest warbler. Luckily, though, its population is increasing: the number of pairs is over 2300 now, up from only about 200 in 1987. Kirtland's Warbler has also expanded its historical Michigan breeding range to include Wisconsin and Ontario. It nests in young stands of Jack Pine that are 1.5–5 meters tall. Plantations of Jack Pine are maintained to provide suitable habitat for this picky bird. Another helpful management practice is controlling the Brown-headed Cowbird population. The cowbird's habit of laying its eggs in other birds' nests is particularly detrimental to a rare species such as the Kirtland's Warbler. Without cowbird control, it is estimated that the endangered Kirtland's Warbler would have been extinct by 1980.

♂ SPRING

Black lores • *broken white eyering* • bluish gray upperparts • dark streaks on back • *yellow throat*, breast and belly • *black streaks or spots on sides* • two thin white wingbars • white undertail coverts • white tail spots • dark legs • (first spring males may be slightly duller overall).

♀ SPRING

Similar to spring male but duller overall. Browner upperparts, less distinct streaks on sides, no black in the lores.

Spring female

REAUME

♂ FIRST FALL
Similar to spring female.

♀ FIRST FALL
Similar to spring female but can be quite brownish above with less distinctive streaks on side and paler yellow underparts.

COMPARE TO
Female Magnolia, Prairie.

LISTEN FOR
A series of fluid, rich notes similar in quality to the Northern Waterthrush.

NATURE NOTES
This species pumps its tail. The male Kirtland's Warbler is quite a persistent singer; one sang 2212 times in one day. The first record of a Kirtland's Warbler was not until 1851 and its breeding grounds were not found until 1903.

This species will eat ripe blueberries and even feed them to its young. Its only known wintering grounds is in the Bahama islands.

RANGE
■ Breeding only
  Wintering only

Setophaga tigrina

Spring male

THE FIRST SPECIMEN of this warbler used to describe the species was taken in Cape May county, New Jersey, in 1811. It may seem like an appropriate name, except that it wasn't seen in Cape May again until 1920! Richard C. Harlow (in Bent, 1953) wrote, "the male Cape May is the tiger of the northwoods in defending his territory. He attacks all birds that come close to the nest, up to the size of the olive-backed thrush (Swainson's Thrush) and is absolutely fearless." The comparison to a tiger also refers to the male's striped breast, which earns it the Latin name *tigrina*. This warbler has a thin beak that curves downward slightly.

♂ SPRING ADULT

Blackish crown • *yellow eyebrow* with some chestnut • *black eyeline* • *chestnut cheek* • yellow throat (may have some chestnut here, too) • *yellow behind cheek* • olive-green back with blackish spots • *yellow rump* • white wing patch • bright yellow breast • white belly and undertail coverts (some light yellow may be on these areas as well) • breast, sides and upper belly *streaked with black* • white tail spots • dark legs.

♂ FIRST SPRING

Slightly duller overall.

Spring female

FAIRBAIRN

♀ SPRING

Dull green crown • yellowish eyebrow • dusky eyeline • yellow throat • *pale yellow behind cheeks* • dull green back with dusky streaks • *yellowish rump* • thin whitish wingbars • yellow breast • whitish belly and undertail coverts • breast and sides streaked with gray. (First spring female can be very dull, with underparts mostly dull white with a yellowish tinge but still has a bright yellowish-olive rump.)

♂ FALL

As spring male but • less black in crown • less chestnut (may be absent) on face.

♀ FALL

As spring female but • yellow behind cheeks is harder to see • upperparts are grayer • less streaking on breast • still has a yellowish-olive rump. (First fall female even duller, yellow may be absent on breast and behind cheeks.)

RANGE	
■	Breeding only
	Wintering only

Fall male

SHUTTERSTOCK/PAUL REEVES PHOTOGRAPHY

COMPARE TO

Yellow-rumped, Pine, Palm, Cerulean, Blackburnian, Bay-breasted, Blackpoll, Tennessee.

LISTEN FOR

A very high-pitched *seet seet seet seet seet*.

NATURE NOTES

The Cape May Warbler's semi-tubular tongue (different from that of other warblers) is used to feed on nectar and fruit juices in its wintering range. It has the largest clutch size recorded for a warbler – nine eggs! One unlucky Cape May Warbler was found in the stomach of a Chuck-will's-widow.

Spring male showing yellow rump

FAIRBAIRN

Fall female; note the yellowish rump and white undertail coverts

SHUTTERSTOCK/AGAMI PHOTO AGENCY

Fall female

FAIRBAIRN

Very dull first fall female

EARLEY

Setophaga cerulea

Spring Male

McCAW

NAMED FOR ITS brilliant cerulean-blue back, this brightly-colored warbler can be surprisingly hard to see. As with the Northern Parula, knowing this warbler's song will definitely help you find it. S. Harmsted Chubb (1919) wrote, "A bird more difficult to observe I have rarely met with. His life seemed to be confined almost entirely to the tops of the tallest deciduous trees, where he would generally feed, with apparent design, on the side most remote from the would-be observer.... Had it not been for the almost incessant singing... the task of identification would have seemed hopeless."

♂ ADULT

Bright blue upperparts • white throat • may have a dark streak on sides of crown • dusky eyeline • black streaking on back • white underparts • dark band across breast • dark streaks on sides • white spots in tail • dark legs. (Fall adult male may have a white eyebrow behind eye.)

♂ FIRST SPRING

Similar but blue not as bright and there is a white eyebrow behind the eye.

♀ SPRING

Light turquoise upperparts with a bluer crown • white or buffy eyebrow • two white wingbars • underparts whitish or slightly buffy • indistinct, blurry streaks on sides. (First spring females may be greenish.)

First spring male — REAUME

Spring female — SHUTTERSTOCK/AGAMI PHOTO AGENCY

♂ FIRST FALL

Similar to spring female but with some dark spots on back, slightly bluer upperparts, whiter underparts.

♀ FALL

Similar to spring adult female but yellower underneath and less distinct streaks on sides. (First fall females are similar to fall adult females but can have quite yellow underparts and olive upperparts • still have white undertail coverts and wingbars.)

Spring female — FAIRBAIRN

COMPARE TO

Blackburnian, Pine, Blackpoll and Bay-breasted in autumn.

LISTEN FOR

A buzzy series of notes that start to rise in pitch and then end in a high buzzy trill *zray zray zray zreeeeeee!*

NATURE NOTES

Because this warbler's preferred habitat is continuous deciduous or mixed forest, it is quite sensitive to habitat fragmentation caused by development.

RANGE
■ Breeding only
  Wintering only

Setophaga americana

Spring male

THE NORTHERN PARULA is one of the smallest warblers but it makes up for its lack of size with its beautiful plumage. It tends not to be as "hyper" as other warblers and so it may be overlooked as it forages in the uppermost branches. As described by Bent (1953), "it creeps along the branches and hops from twig to twig, often clinging to the under side of a cluster like a chickadee, an action that led some of the early writers to refer to it as a small titmouse." The name *Parula* does indeed mean little titmouse or chickadee. It is especially important to know this warbler's song, as that is often the only clue of its presence.

♂ SPRING

Blue head • black lores • *broken white eyering* • *bicolored beak* • *yellow throat* • blue back and rump • olive-green patch on back • bold white wingbars • yellow breast • white belly and undertail coverts • *a band across the breast* is usually made up of black and chestnut • white tail spots.

♀ SPRING

Similar to the male but duller overall, with • dusky lores • bluish-gray upper-parts • breast band is absent or a very light chestnut.

Female

REAUME

Singing male

McCAW

RANGE
Breeding only
Wintering only

Fall male

♂♀ FALL

Upperparts a bit greener than in spring, *broken eyering* bigger • breast band less distinct (not present at all in first fall female).

COMPARE TO

Nashville and Magnolia in autumn.

LISTEN FOR

A buzzy ascending trill that usually drops at the end: ***zeeeeeeeeeee-up***.

NATURE NOTES

In the northern parts of this warbler's breeding range, it usually makes its nest in hanging *Usnea* or *Ramalina* lichens. In the south, it uses hanging Spanish Moss.

Male showing its chickadee-like foraging behavior

First spring female

Fall; all plumages show the green patch on the back

Setophaga magnolia

Spring male

ANOTHER NAME RELATED to the warblers' migration: Alexander Wilson saw one in a Magnolia tree along the Mississippi River, far from its summer and winter homes. He actually gave it a former English name, "Black and Yellow Warbler," because of its showy plumage. Bent (1953) wrote, "…and it seems to me that in the Magnolia warbler, more than in any one of the many beautiful species of American wood warblers, are the best combined daintiness of attire with pleasing combinations and contrasts of often brilliant colors."

NOTE

Yellow rump is present in all plumages.

♂ SPRING

Black cheeks and lores • gray crown • white eyebrow behind eye only • broken white eyering • *yellow throat* • mostly black back • *large white wing patch* • *yellow breast and belly with thick black streaks* • white undertail coverts • short white tail spots leave a distinctive black band on the end of the tail • dark legs.

♂ FIRST SPRING

Male is slightly duller overall compared to spring adult male and has more greenish feather edges in the black of back.

♀ SPRING

Duller overall than spring male with • grayer cheeks and lores • olive-green back with black spots • black streaking on breast thinner.

Spring female

SHUTTERSTOCK/AGAMI PHOTO AGENCY

♀ FIRST SPRING

Duller than spring adult female and may have • even grayer cheeks and lores • indistinct eyebrow and broken eyering • wingbars instead of a wing patch • less black streaking on underparts.

♂ FALL ADULT

Similar to dull first spring female except for • mostly gray head • little or no eyebrow • full whitish eyering • may have gray on breast • less black streaking on underparts, very little on breast.

♀ FALL   ♂ FIRST FALL

Slightly duller than fall adult male. First fall with a grayish band across the breast. (First fall female may have no spots on back and very little streaking on underparts.)

RANGE
■ Breeding only
  Wintering only

Tail spots leaving black band at the end of the tail

SHUTTERSTOCK/PAUL REEVES PHOTOGRAPHY

COMPARE TO

Canada, Kirtland's and Yellow-rumped in spring; first fall Prairie, Canada, and Nashville in autumn.

LISTEN FOR

A musical series of notes such as **weety weety weet chew**.

NATURE NOTES

Most Magnolia Warblers fly across the Gulf of Mexico during spring and fall migration. As with other warblers, Magnolia Warblers migrate at night. They will, however, fly in the early morning to make corrections if they were blown off course by high winds during the night.

SHUTTERSTOCK/AGAMI PHOTO AGENCY

Preening spring male showing yellow rump and tail spots

Fall

Spring female

Fall

Spring male

REAUME

CHAPMAN (1907) WROTE, "Bay-breasts and Blackpolls alike are rather big … and both have an almost vireo-like leisureliness of movement." This is a great description of these warblers' slowish actions. The male Bay-breasted Warbler is quite unlike any other warbler in its spring plumage. This species may also pump its tail, but not as often or as noticeably as the Palm Warbler.

♂ SPRING ADULT

Black lores, forehead and cheeks • *reddish chestnut throat, crown, breast and sides* • *buffy patch behind cheek* • gray back and rump with black streaks • two bold white wingbars • whitish or pale buffy belly and undertail coverts • usually dark legs • white spots in tail. (First spring male may have some gray in the cheeks and less chestnut on breast and sides.)

♀ SPRING ADULT

Similar to male except for • less *chestnut in crown* • *buffy or whitish cheeks with dark mottling* • throat may be whitish or light chestnut • *less chestnut on sides and breast* • back and rump have an olive tinge with less streaking. (First spring female may have very little chestnut overall.)

♂ FALL ADULT

Olive crown • dusky lores and eyeline • indistinct yellowish eyebrow • olive back with black streaks • whitish or buffy throat • *buffy belly and undertail coverts* • *light chestnut on sides* • grayish-olive rump • *two white wingbars* • may have some chestnut on throat or crown. (First fall male is similar but may lack

Spring female · SHUTTERSTOCK/AGAMI PHOTO AGENCY

Duller spring female · FAIRBAIRN

any chestnut, may have a deeper buff on sides.)

♀ FALL ADULT

Is similar to fall male but with no chestnut, may have a deeper buff on sides. (First fall female is similar but with less streaking on back and less distinctive markings on face. May have some light streaking on sides of breast.)

COMPARE TO

In autumn, Blackpoll, Pine, female Blackburnian, Chestnut-sided.

Fall · SHUTTERSTOCK/PAUL REEVES PHOTOGRAPHY

LISTEN FOR

A high-pitched series of notes that increase in intensity *see-see-see-see-see*.

NATURE NOTES

Tends to feed in the middle of conifer trees, near the trunk, on its breeding grounds. Population densities are at their highest during spruce budworm outbreaks. One Bay-breasted Warbler was seen being caught and eaten by a Cattle Egret on its wintering grounds.

RANGE
■ Breeding only
☐ Wintering only

Spring male

McCAW

HERE IS A BIRD whose bright Halloween colors have to be seen on a clear spring morning to be believed. The male Blackburnian Warbler's orange throat appears to glow, giving it such previous names as "Firethroat" and "Torchbird." Bent (1953) wrote, "Blackburnian seems to be a doubly appropriate name, for its upperparts are largely black and its throat burns like a brilliant orange flame amid the dark foliage of the hemlocks and spruces. A glimpse of such a brilliant gem, flashing out from its somber surroundings, is fairly startling." This warbler is actually named after Anna Blackburne, who was a biologist in the late 1700s.

♂ SPRING

Orange eyebrow • *orange throat* • *orange behind cheek* • *white wing patch* • broken orange eyering • black crown with orange spot • black cheek • orange breast (fading to yellow towards belly) • black streaks on sides • white or very light yellow belly and undertail coverts • black back with a whitish line • black rump • dark legs • large white spots in tail.

♀ SPRING

Similar to male except for orange replaced by yellow-orange • black replaced by brownish-gray • two white wingbars • streaking on back as well as a pale line.

Spring female   REAUME

The brilliant breast of the spring male   FAIRBAIRN

♂♀ FALL

Similar to spring adults but slightly duller overall with less orange. (First fall female can be very dull with almost a whitish throat and the cheek is surrounded by light yellow or buff.)

COMPARE TO

Fall Cerulean, Bay-breasted, Blackpoll & Cape May.

LISTEN FOR

A very high, variable series of notes with the last one slurring upwards and almost disappearing at the end: *seat seat seat ti-ti-ti zeeeee*.

NATURE NOTES

The Blackburnian Warbler's song is so high that many birders can't hear the end notes and some can't hear the song at all. For comparison, the high-pitched song of the Black-throated Green Warbler is between 4 and 6 kHz, whereas the even higher Blackburnian's song is between 4 and 11 kHz.

Fall female   SHUTTERSTOCK/C. HAMILTON

RANGE
■ Breeding only
  Wintering only

Setophaga petechia

Male

"A BIT OF FEATHERED sunshine. In his plumes dwells the gold of the sun, in his voice his brightness and good cheer." Here Chapman (1907) has captured the spirit of the well-known Yellow Warbler, once called the Summer Yellow Bird. It is often overlooked because of being common, but its abundance makes it a good warbler to watch for courtship and nesting behaviors. Knowing it by sight and sound can help with identification of other, similar warblers.

♂ SPRING

All yellow head · greenish-yellow nape, back and rump · wing feathers edged in yellow · *yellow underparts with reddish streaks* on breast and sides · *yellow spots in tail* · light or pinkish legs.

♀ SPRING

Same as spring male but with · greenish-yellow crown · little or no reddish streaks on breast.

♂ FALL

The same as spring but with more greenish-yellow in crown and less reddish streaking on breast. (First fall males resemble adult spring females.)

♀ FALL

Slightly duller than in spring. (First fall females lack reddish breast streaks and may have a thin light eyering.)

Female   SHUTTERSTOCK/AGAMI PHOTO AGENCY

First year females can be quite dull   SMALL

COMPARE TO

Orange-crowned, first year female Hooded, female Wilson's.

LISTEN FOR

A series of clear high whistles such as *sweet sweet shredded wheat*.

NATURE NOTES

The amount of red streaking is not age-related in adult birds. Those with more red are often more aggressive in their territorial defense, and other Yellow Warbler males are more aggressive towards these individuals. The Latin name *petechia* means "purplish spot" and is derived from a medical term used to describe a purplish or reddish rash, like the spots on the male Yellow Warbler's breast. Yellow Warblers are very early fall migrants, with many leaving eastern North America by the end of August. Brown-headed Cowbirds lay their eggs in this warbler's nests more than with any other bird species except for the Song Sparrow. One defense the Yellow Warbler has against this is to build another nest floor on top of the intruding egg where it will become too cold and die. This may be repeated every time a new cowbird egg is laid. The record is six layers of floors in a single nest!

RANGE

■ Breeding only
■ Resident year round
   Wintering only

Setophaga pensylvanica

Spring male

THIS IS A WARBLER that has expanded in numbers because of the extensive deforestation of eastern North America. Frank Chapman (1907) writes that "the Chestnut-sided Warbler, for example, considered by Wilson and Audubon to be a rare species, is now abundant and we may believe that this change in numbers is due largely to the development of those scrub and second growths in which this bird delights." It is also a warbler that in autumn looks quite different from the way it does in the spring. It often holds its tail at an angle upwards from its back and may droop its wings; here's where behavior and overall shape can be used to help you recognize it in the autumn after making spring observations.

Spring female

SHUTTERSTOCK/AGAMI PHOTO AGENCY

♂ SPRING

Black eyeline • *black moustache* • *yellow crown* • *white throat* • greenish back and rump with black streaks • yellowish wingbars • white underparts • a broad *chestnut line* extends from the moustache along the sides of the breast to the flanks • white tail spots • dark legs. (First spring male duller overall with black on face less distinct and chestnut on sides not as extensive; crown is a greener yellow.)

♀ SPRING

Same as spring male except for • duller overall • less distinct eyeline • lime-green crown • less chestnut on sides. (First spring female has little or no chestnut on sides and limited black on the face.)

♂ FALL ADULT

Same as spring male except for • no eyeline or moustache • lime-green crown • *gray cheeks* • *white eyering* • white throat • still has chestnut on sides.

RANGE

- ■ Breeding only
- Wintering only

Fall

♀ FALL   ♂ FIRST FALL

Similar to fall adult male except for less chestnut on sides (possibly none on some individuals) · less distinct spots on back. (First fall female even duller with no chestnut on sides.)

COMPARE TO

Fall females may be like fall Blackpoll or Bay-breasted.

LISTEN FOR

A whistled *pleased pleased pleased to meetcha*.

NATURE NOTES

Tends to search the undersides of leaves for food. This warbler may bury intruding Brown-headed Cowbird eggs in the floor of its nest like the Yellow Warbler.

Fall

First spring female

REAUME

Male with less chestnut

McCAW

Setophaga striata

Spring male

AT FIRST GLANCE, the Blackpoll Warbler looks surprisingly like a Black-capped Chickadee. Both have the black cap or "poll," but the Blackpoll Warbler has a white throat, black streaks on its sides and wingbars. This is one of the last warblers to arrive in the spring. In the fall, it is easily confused with Bay-breasted and Pine Warblers. (See Fall Comparison 2, pages 124–125.)

♂ SPRING

Black cap and malar stripe • white cheeks and throat • gray upperparts with black streaks • two white wingbars • white underparts • *black streaks on sides* • usually has yellowish or pinkish legs in spring • white tail spots.

♀ SPRING

Greenish-gray crown and upperparts with dark streaks • *dusky eyeline* • light eyebrow • blurry malar stripe may be present • underparts white or yellowish with *thin streaks on the sides* and sometimes the breast • leg color as above.

♂ FALL

Olive-green crown and upperparts with thin black streaks • blurry dark eyeline • yellowish eyebrow • two white wingbars • usually yellowish underparts with contrasting *white undertail coverts* • thin streaks on sides. (First fall male has less extensive streaks on sides.)

♀ FALL

Similar to fall male except for • little streaking on crown, less streaking on sides, may have a slight yellow tinge to undertail coverts. (First fall female is similar to fall adult female but may have

Spring female — SHUTTERSTOCK/AGAMI PHOTO AGENCY

Fall — SHUTTERSTOCK/AGAMI PHOTO AGENCY

very little streaking on sides.) (First fall birds may have dark legs but usually have yellow on the back of the legs and soles of the feet.)

COMPARE TO

Black-and-white, female Cerulean in spring; Bay-breasted, Pine in autumn.

LISTEN FOR

A very high-pitched series of notes *see-see-see-see-see-see* that may increase in volume in the middle.

NATURE NOTES

This warbler has a remarkable fall migration route. It may fly over the Atlantic Ocean from the southeastern coast of the Maritime provinces and New England to the north shore of South America – non-stop! It is estimated that they may fly without stopping for over 72 hours and lose 50% of their body weight.

Fall; note the pale feet and legs — McCAW

RANGE
■ Breeding only
  Wintering only

Black-throated Blue Warbler

Setophaga caerulescens

Male

ONE MAY MORNING when I was 15, I saw a male Black-throated Blue Warbler in a mulberry tree in my backyard. My interest in warblers and subsequently in all birds made a big leap that day because of this beautiful warbler's markings. Its black throat and blue upperparts make the male one of the easiest warblers to identify, but in contrast, the female can be one of the most difficult for the beginner. The white spot on her wing is distinctive but may not be present on first-year females. The male and female are so different that both Alexander Wilson and J.J. Audubon thought they were separate species!

♂ SPRING

Blue upperparts • black face and throat • white wing patch • white underparts • black sides • light to dark brown legs • white tail spots. (First spring male a bit duller overall and has greenish-brown flight feathers.)

♀ SPRING

Thin light eyebrow • broken eyering • brownish-green upperparts, tinged with blue • cheek a bit darker • *white wing patch* • buffy underparts, whiter on belly • gray tail spots. (First spring female has a smaller or no wing patch.)

Female   FAIRBAIRN

First spring male   McCAW

FALL

Similar to spring except first fall male is slightly duller overall with greenish flight feathers, first fall female may be browner than adult and lack white wing patch.

COMPARE TO

Females to Tennessee, Orange-crowned, first year female Pine.

LISTEN FOR

A buzzy *I'm so lay-zeeee* with the last note rising in pitch.

NATURE NOTES

There is one record of a Black-throated Blue Warbler that had male plumage on its left side and female plumage on its right side. So, depending on what side you saw, it would be either easy or difficult to identify!

First spring female   SHUTTERSTOCK/AGAMI PHOTO AGENCY

RANGE	
■	Breeding only
	Wintering only

Palm Warbler

Setophaga palmarum

Spring "Western" Palm Warbler

ITS HABIT OF PUMPING its tail puts the Palm Warbler into perpetual motion. Maynard wrote, "The constant watchfulness of these birds, which is exhibited by every movement, is necessary for their existence for they usually inhabit open places where they are in constant danger from the attacks of enemies" (Studer, 1881). This warbler got its latin name, *palmarum*, from the palm groves in which it was first found during the winter on Hispaniola. The old name of "Yellow Red-poll Warbler" seems more fitting, at least for one subspecies. There are two distinct subspecies of this warbler, the "Yellow" Palm Warbler and the "Western" Palm Warbler. The "Yellow" Palm Warbler is more often seen on the Atlantic Coast.

♂ SPRING "WESTERN"

Chestnut crown • yellow eyebrow • dark eyeline • *yellow throat •* whitish broken eye-ring • thin moustache • grayish-brown back and with an olive-yellow rump • indistinct wingbars • yellow breast • whitish belly • *yellow undertail coverts • breast streaked with chestnut brown lines.*

♂ SPRING "YELLOW"

Similar to "Western" but brighter overall with a yellow broken eyering, *all yellow underparts* and *reddish streaks on breast.*

Spring "Yellow" Palm Warbler

Fall; note the yellow undertail coverts and yellowish rump

♀ SPRING

A bit duller than the males with some first spring females not having a chestnut cap or yellow in breast • dark legs • white spots in tail.

FALL

Brownish crown with varying amounts of chestnut (first fall female may have no chestnut in crown) • whitish or buffy eyebrow • whitish throat • whitish or pale yellow underparts except for bright yellow undertail coverts. ("Yellow" Palm Warbler tends to have yellower underparts than "Western.")

Fall   FAIRBAIRN

COMPARE TO

Cape May, the waterthrushes, in fall with Yellow-rumped, Orange-crowned.

LISTEN FOR

A flat, buzzy trill.

NATURE NOTES

In the Canadian Shield part of its Ontario range, there are usually less than 10 pairs per 100 km², but in the Hudson Bay lowlands there are up to 272 pairs per km².

RANGE

■ Breeding only
   Wintering only

Pine Warbler

Setophaga pinus

Spring male

HERE IS A WARBLER that has been named well. Gerald Thayer (in Chapman, 1907) wrote, "Never was a bird more aptly named than the Pine Warbler. Except when migrating, it sticks to pine woods as a cockle-bur sticks to a dog's tail." These warblers are bulky-looking and their movements are almost sluggish when compared to most other warbler species. The first-year females can be very dull in coloration and may thus cause confusion, especially in the fall. It can be challenging to distinguish this warbler from fall Blackpoll and Bay-breasted Warblers (see Fall Comparison 2, pages 124–125).

♂ SPRING

Olive-green crown and cheek • *yellow throat* • thin yellow eyebrow • thin broken yellow eyering • slightly dusky lores • yellow breast • *white belly and undertail coverts* • olive-green back and rump • *whitish wingbars* • variable *dusky streaks on sides of breast* • legs dark • white tail spots.

♀ SPRING

Similar to the male except for • less yellow on breast and not as bright • usually *no streaks on sides*.

♀ FIRST SPRING & FIRST FALL

Very *brownish overall* with fainter wingbars • whitish underparts with a light brown wash • only a hint of yellow on breast.

Spring female — SMALL

Fall — REAUME

FALL ADULT ♂ FIRST FALL

Similar to spring adults but slightly duller overall.

COMPARE TO

Yellow-throated Vireo in spring; Blackpoll, Bay-breasted, Tennessee, Prairie, Cape May in autumn.

LISTEN FOR

A musical Chipping Sparrow-like trill.

NATURE NOTES

This warbler may come to bird feeders for suet. It is a short-distance migrant that winters in the southeastern states, though there are records of them overwintering in the Great Lakes region. This warbler occasionally buries Brown-headed Cowbird eggs in the floor of its nest as does the Yellow Warbler.

Yellow-throated Vireo (for comparison) — EARLEY

RANGE
- ■ Breeding only
- ▨ Resident year round
- Wintering only

Yellow-rumped Warbler

Setophaga coronata

Spring male

SMALL

SHOWING A WHITE throat, the "Myrtle" form of the Yellow-rumped Warbler is very common in eastern North America and is often the first warbler seen in the spring in northern areas. In fact, this is the only warbler that can regularly be found overwintering as far north as the Great Lakes region. The western North American "Audubon's" form of the Yellow-rumped Warbler sports a yellow throat and is rare in eastern North America. The Latin name *coronata* means "crowned" and refers to the yellow patch on this warbler's head that gave it the former names of "Golden-crowned Flycatcher" and "Yellow-crowned Warbler." The yellow patches on the Yellow-rumped Warbler appear to be very important in courtship, as Forbush (1929) describes: "the males begin their courtship of the females, following them about and displaying their beauties by fluffing out the feathers of their sides, raising their wings and erecting the feathers of the crown, so as to exhibit to the full their beautiful black and yellow markings."

Spring female

SHUTTERSTOCK/AGAMI PHOTO AGENCY

NOTE

Yellow rump is present in all plumages.

♂ SPRING

Bluish-gray crown and nape • yellow patch on crown • black cheeks and lores • *white throat* • white broken eyebrow • white broken eyering • bluish-gray back with black streaks • *two white wingbars* • white underparts • mottled black breast that extends into streaks on flanks • *yellow patch on sides of breast* • white spots in tail • dark legs.

♀ SPRING ADULT

Duller than spring male with brownish-gray upperparts instead of bluish-gray • browner cheeks • smaller yellow crown patch • streaking instead of thicker mottling of black on breast. (First spring females may have little streaking on breast.)

♂ FALL ADULT

Similar to spring female except for
• duller eyebrow and broken eyering
• a buffy wash on breast • lower back and uppertail coverts may still be the spring male's bluish-gray.

RANGE

■ Breeding only
■ Resident year round
  Wintering only

Fall

REAUME

♀ FALL ADULT ♂ FIRST FALL

Slightly duller overall than fall adult male with less streaking on underparts and more buffy wash on underparts.

♀ FIRST FALL

Can be very brown with a buffy throat • very fine streaking on the upperparts and underparts • may lack yellow crown and yellow side patches • may have very thin buffy wingbars.

COMPARE TO

Magnolia in spring; Cape May and Pine in autumn.

LISTEN FOR

A variable slow and jingling trill.

NATURE NOTES

This warbler uses special enzymes to digest the waxes in bayberries, one of which is called wax myrtle; thus the

Spring male showing yellow rump

SHUTTERSTOCK/M. LEONARD PHOTOGRAPHY

name "Myrtle" Warbler. Bayberries allow Yellow-rumped Warblers to stay as far north as Nova Scotia in winter. The "Myrtle" form and the "Audubon's" form interbreed in the Canadian Rockies. The Yellow-rumped Warbler is the most abundant warbler in Canada.

Female

SHUTTERSTOCK/FOTOREQUEST

SHUTTERSTOCK/AGAMI PHOTO AGENCY

Spring male "Audubon's" Yellow-rumped Warbler

SHUTTERSTOCK/VAGABOND54

Fall "Audubon's"; note the buffy yellow throat

Setophaga dominica

"THE HABITS AND manners of this splendid little bird are not consistent with the shape and construction of his bill, his ways being those of the Creepers or Titmouse, while the peculiarities of his bill rank him with the Warblers" (Studer, 1881). The Yellow-throated Warbler puts its longish bill to good use as it creeps along branches much like a nuthatch (or a Black-and-white Warbler). It also probes for insects in pine cones and bundles of pine needles.

♂ SPRING ADULT

Broken white eyering, white (may be yellow near beak) eyebrow • *black eyeline and cheek* • black forecrown and streaks of black in the rest of the crown • *white patch behind cheek* • bluish-gray upperparts • two white wingbars • *yellow throat and upper breast* • white lower breast, belly and undertail coverts • *black streaks on sides* • white tail spots • dark legs.

ALL OTHER PLUMAGES

Similar to spring adult male, but slightly duller overall, females with less black in the crown.

COMPARE TO

Female and fall male Blackburnian Warbler.

LISTEN FOR

A series of thin, down-slurred whistles that descends in pitch. Quality is similar to the Indigo Bunting.

SHUTTERSTOCK/RAY HENNESSY

SHUTTERSTOCK/PAUL REEVES PHOTOGRAPHY

Visiting a suet feeder

SHUTTERSTOCK/RAY HENNESSY

This species can move nuthatch-like on tree trunks

NATURE NOTES

This species has hybridized with the Northern Parula. The hybrid is called the "Sutton's Warbler" and it looks similar to a Yellow-throated Warbler, but with no streaking on the sides and some green on the back. The Yellow-throated Warbler sometimes comes to bird feeders.

RANGE

■ Breeding only
▨ Resident year round
☐ Wintering only

Setophaga discolor

Spring male

THIS WARBLER, LIKE the Palm Warbler, pumps its tail regularly, which can be a good aid in identification, especially when looking at first-fall individuals. In regards to its name, Ludlow Griscom (1979) writes, "'Prairie' is misleading; Scrub Warbler would be better, for such habitat is the home of this exquisite little bird. I have long thought it one of the most appealing of the family, a close view of a high-plumaged male being as lovely a picture of animated nature as one could see."

♂ SPRING

Yellow eyebrow · *black eyeline joined to a black moustache that curves across the cheek leaving a yellow patch under the eye* · olive-green crown · *yellow throat* · olive-green upperparts with chestnut streaking on back · yellow wingbars · yellow breast and belly with *black streaking* on sides · lighter yellow on undertail coverts · large white tail spots · dark legs. (First spring male slightly duller overall with black on face less distinct and less chestnut on back.)

♀ SPRING

Same as spring male but with · most or all of the black facial pattern replaced with olive-green · less chestnut on back · less black streaking on breast. (First spring female is the same but may have some white on the throat.)

Spring female

FAIRBAIRN

Fall

SHUTTERSTOCK/CHRISTOPHER UNSWORTH

♂ FALL

Same as spring male but with less chestnut on back and less black streaking on sides of breast. (First fall male usually resembles adult female, but may have flecks of black in facial pattern and more chestnut on back.)

♀ FALL

As spring adult female but with less distinct facial pattern and less chestnut on back.

♀ FIRST FALL

As fall adult female but can be much duller overall with a grayish head, whitish eyebrow, whitish throat, less streaking on sides of breast, indistinct wingbars, whitish undertail coverts and no chestnut on back. (This can be a tough one, but it still has a hint of the Prairie facial pattern.)

COMPARE TO

Adult male Pine, Magnolia and Palm in autumn.

LISTEN FOR

A series of buzzes that rise in pitch.

NATURE NOTES

Prairie Warbler numbers have declined in parts of their range due to the succession of scrublands into mature forest.

RANGE
- ■ Breeding only
- ■ Resident year round
-   Wintering only

Black-throated Green Warbler

Setophaga virens

Spring male

THIS WARBLER'S VOICE is a distinctive sound in the northern woods. Bent (1953) writes, "The song has been written as 'trees, trees, murmuring trees,' appropriate words that seem to call vividly to mind the pretty little bird in its sylvan haunts and its delicious and soothing voice." The Black-throated Green Warbler's yellow cheeks make it one of the warblers that is not too hard to identify, whether it be spring, summer or fall.

♂ SPRING

Yellow eyebrow and cheeks • black throat • olive-green crown and eyeline • olive-green back and rump • white wingbars • may have some faint black streaks on back • black breast with black streaks on sides of breast • white (or sometimes yellowish) belly • some yellow between undertail coverts and belly • white undertail coverts may have some black lines • large white tail spots • dark legs. (First spring male may have some white on throat.)

♀ SPRING

Similar to spring male but with a yellowish throat • white in the black of the breast (some have more black than others). (First spring female may have no black on throat or breast and only thin streaks on the sides of the breast.)

♂ FALL

Same as spring male but with white in the black of throat and breast. (First fall male has more white in throat than the adult.)

Spring female   SHUTTERSTOCK/AGAMI PHOTO AGENCY

Fall   FAIRBAIRN

♀ FALL

Has more white in throat than the spring adult. (First fall female as first spring female but even less black on sides.)

LISTEN FOR

A high, buzzy *zee zee zee zoo zee* or *zoo zee zoo zoo zee, (trees trees murmuring trees)*.

NATURE NOTES

One male sang 466 songs in an hour! In parts of its range where several other *Setophaga* warblers breed, Black-throated Green Warblers are more specialized foragers than in areas where few *Setophaga* warblers are present. This is because of increased competition for food resources where more *Setophaga* species live; each species has its own special niche to fill.

First fall female   SHUTTERSTOCK/RAY HENNESSY

RANGE	
■	Breeding only
	Wintering only

Cardellina canadensis

Spring male   McCAW

THE SPECTACLES OF the Canada Warbler tend to give it a surprised look. Gerald Thayer (in Chapman, 1907) describes it as "a sprightly, wide-awake, fly-snapping Warbler, vivid in movement and in song; clearly marked and brightly colored." It was once called the "Canadian Fly-catcher" because of its feeding habits. It is often found on or near the ground, where its active foraging behavior may reveal its presence.

♂ SPRING

Grayish-blue upperparts • some black spots on crown • *yellow eyebrow joining to whitish eyering to make "spectacles"* • *black lores and sideburns* • *yellow throat, breast and belly* • black streaks on breast form *a necklace* • *white undertail coverts* • pinkish legs • no tail spots. (First spring males may have less black streaking.)

♀ SPRING

Similar to spring adult male but duller overall with little black on face and blurrier streaks on breast. (First spring female similar to spring adult females but with grayer streaks on breast.)

♂ FALL

Similar to spring but black markings less distinct.

FAIRBAIRN

First spring female

♀ FALL   ♀ FIRST FALL

Are slightly duller than spring female.
(First fall female usually lacks all black;
grayish streaks on breast may be
very indistinct.)

COMPARE TO

Magnolia, Nashville, Kentucky.

LISTEN FOR

An initial chip followed by a variable
series of musical notes.

NATURE NOTES

The male is known to offer food
to its eggs; this behavior is called
"anticipatory feeding."

McCAW

Spring female

REAUME

Spring male

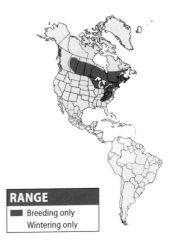

RANGE

■ Breeding only
  Wintering only

Cardellina pusilla

Spring male REAUME

BENT (1953) WROTE, "Whenever we meet the little bird our attention is sure to be drawn to it by its bright song, and then the eye is caught by the quick sprightliness of its demeanor, and a flash of sunny gold." The Wilson's Warbler's black cap makes it look as if it were wearing a yarmulke or had a brush-cut. Chapman (1907) describes its tail movements as "sharply flip-flip-flipping for many seconds together, and again it will be perfectly still for a longer time." This warbler has a longish tail for its size and is one of the smallest warblers, *pusilla* meaning "very small."

♂ SPRING

Black cap • yellow forehead, eyebrow and throat • greenish tinge to cheeks • olive-green upperparts • yellow underparts • pinkish legs • no tail spots. (First spring male may have some greenish feathers in the rear part of black cap.)

♀ SPRING

Similar to spring male but has less or no black in cap.

FALL

Birds with a cap often have greenish feathers in the black.

Spring female   SMALL

Fall male   McCAW

COMPARE TO

Yellow, Hooded, Orange-crowned.

LISTEN FOR

A fast, musical series of notes that drops in pitch at the end *chee-chee-chee-chee-chee-chet-chet-chet*.

NATURE NOTES

The flycatching habits of the Wilson's Warbler earned it the older name of "Green Black-capped Fly-catcher."

Fall male   SHUTTERSTOCK/NICK PECKER

First fall female   EARLEY

RANGE

■ Breeding only
Wintering only

Vagrants & Stragglers

OVER 50 SPECIES of warblers have been recorded in the United States and Canada. In eastern North America, the following western and southwestern warbler species are not common occurrences but have occurred here: some species may show up almost every year and some species may have only ever been recorded a few times.

Lucy's Warbler

Leiothlypis luciae

This small warbler normally lives along rivers and streams in the southwestern parts of the United States. It is a grayish bird with a rufous rump and rufous spot on its crown.

SMALL

Virginia's Warbler

Leiothlypis virginiae

This warbler's regular summer range is in the southwestern states. It is similar in appearance to the Nashville Warbler but has a grayer back and usually has a whitish throat and less yellow on the breast.

SMALL

MacGillivray's Warbler

Geothlypis tolmiei

This warbler is very similar to the Mourning Warbler. Some Mourning Warblers may have a thin broken eyering and dusky lores, so identification can be difficult. This species breeds in the western part of North America.

SHUTTERSTOCK/PUNKBIRDR

Tropical Parula

Setophaga pitiayumi

This brightly colored warbler is very similar to the Northern Parula except for its all-dark face and lack of a dark band on its breast. They inhabit a few places in central and southern Texas south into Mexico.

SHUTTERSTOCK/AFONSO FARIAS

Grace's Warbler

Setophaga graciae

A warbler of the southwestern states, this species resembles a Yellow-throated Warbler but with a shorter beak and more yellow on its face. It is also missing the Yellow-throated Warbler's white patch behind its cheek.

SMALL

Black-throated Gray Warbler

Setophaga nigrescens

SHUTTERSTOCK/AGAMI PHOTO AGENCY

Similar in appearance to the Black-and-white Warbler but without a white median crown stripe or white stripes on its back. The Black-throated Gray Warbler's black cheek patch and black throat separate it from the male Blackpoll Warbler. Its breeding range includes southern B.C., Alberta and south to Mexico.

Townsend's Warbler

Setophaga townsendi

SHUTTERSTOCK/AGAMI PHOTO AGENCY

A close relative of the Black-throated Green Warbler, the Townsend's Warbler has a dark cheek patch that separates it from its eastern cousin. Its breeding range includes southwestern Alaska and Yukon Territory and much of B.C. and the northwestern states.

Hermit Warbler

Setophaga occidentalis

SHUTTERSTOCK/PUNKBIRDR

Another relative of the Black-throated Green Warbler, the Hermit Warbler has more yellow on its face, a much grayer back and very little streaking on its sides. Its breeding range is mainly in the Pacific states.

The warbler is similar to the Black-throated Green Warbler, but it has more yellow on its cheeks and more black overall. Golden-cheeked Warblers breed in central Texas.

SMALL

Red-faced Warbler

Cardellina rubifrons

This distinctive-looking warbler is a bird of Arizona and New Mexico. Though it looks very different, it is most closely related to Canada and Wilson's Warblers.

SMALL

Painted Redstart

Myioborus pictus

The only warbler in this book with a solid bright red lower breast, the Painted Redstart breeds in the extreme southwestern states and Mexico. This species has wandered to places such as Minnesota, Ohio, Michigan, New York and Ontario.

EARLEY

What can I do to help warblers?

To learn about habitat management and endangered species, I suggest going on a Kirtland's Warbler tour in Mio or Grayling, Michigan.

AFTER ENJOYING THEIR beautiful colors and seeing them interact with their environment, you may be wondering what you can do to help warblers. Well, the fact that you bought this book has already helped; your interest alone can be very beneficial to all of nature. By learning more about warblers, you have become even more connected to the natural world around you. When you share your interest with others, the growing support for wildlife and their varied habitats increases.

To be more active, you could give support to national, provincial and state parks and conservation areas, as well as to naturalist groups. Organizations such as FLAP (Fatal Light Awareness Program), www.flap.org, work to prevent nighttime migrants such as warblers from flying into lit city buildings. Not only do its members go around the streets of downtown Toronto before dawn to save injured migrating birds, they also have encouraged many big city businesses to turn off their lights at night to decrease the number of migrant fatalities each year.

If you live near a swampy or wet area, you can build nest boxes that could be used by the Prothonotary Warbler. These warblers prefer boxes in the shade that are 1.5 to 2 m high with an entrance hole that is 29 mm in diameter. Nest box plans are available from a variety of sources such as local naturalist groups, nature stores and the Wildlife Service.

Right: A male and female Prothonotary Warbler check out a nest box.

REAUME

References

THERE ARE MANY helpful references that provide a lot of information on warblers. *Peterson Field Guides: Warblers,* by Jon Dunn and Kimball Garrett, is a must for anyone who wants to delve into more detail. It includes plates (paintings) and some photographs and covers all of North America's warbler species. As well, *Warblers of the Americas: An Identification Guide,* by Jon Curson, David Quinn and David Beadle, has concise text and incredible plates of all the American Wood-Warblers, from the Northwest Territories to central South America. The Cornell Lab of Ornithology: Birds of the World website includes heaps of information that has been collected by the scientific community on warblers and their natural history.

American Warblers: An Ecological and Behavioral Perspective by D. H. Morse, 1989, Harvard University Press.

The Audubon Society Encyclopedia of North American Birds by John K. Terres, 1991, Wings Books.

The Birder's Handbook by Ehrlich, Dobkin and Wheye, 1988, Fireside/Simon and Schuster Inc.

The Birds of Canada - revised edition by W. Earl Godfrey, 1986, National Museums of Canada.

Bird Sounds of Canada, by Monty Brigham, Canadian Museum of Nature.

Check-list of North American Birds, 1998, The American Ornithologists' Union.

Cornell Lab of Ornithology: Birds of the World, www.birdsoftheworld.org /bow/home

The Dictionary of American Bird Names, revised edition by E.A. Choate, 1985, Harvard Common Press.

Field Guide to the Birds of North America by the National Geographic Society, 1987.

Field Guide to Warblers by Donald and Lillian Stokes, 2004, Little, Brown and Company.

Life Histories of North American Wood Warblers edited by A.C. Bent, 1953, U.S. National Museum.

Nest Boxes for Prothonotaries by L. Rizzo, Birder's World, April 1994.

Peterson Field Guides: Advance Birding by Kenn Kaufman, 1990, Houghton Mifflin Company.

Peterson Field Guides: Eastern Birds by R.T. Peterson, 1984, Houghton-Mifflin.

Peterson Field Guides: Warblers by Dunn and Garrett, 1997, Houghton Mifflin.

Peterson Natural History Companions: Lives of North American Birds by Kenn Kaufman, 1996, Houghton Mifflin.

Seasonal Status of Birds: Point Pelee National Park and Vicinity compiled by J.R. Graham, 1996.

Studers Popular Ornithology: The Birds of North America edited by J. H. Studer, 1881, Harrison House.

The Sibley Guide to Birds by D.A. Sibley, 2014, Knopf Doubleday Publishing Group.

The Warbler Guide by Stephenson and Whittle, 2013, Princeton University Press.

The Warblers of North America by F.M. Chapman, 1907, D. Appleton and Company.

The Warblers of America by L. Griscom, 1979, Doubleday and Company Inc.

Warblers of the Americas: An Identification Guide by Curson, Quinn and Beadle, 1994, Houghton Mifflin.

Watching Warblers Video by Michael Male and Judy Fieth, 1996, Blue Earth Films.

Wood Warbler's World by H.H. Harrison, 1984, Simon and Schuster Inc.

Apps:
- Larkwire
- Merlin
- eBird
- iNaturalist

Sound Resources:
- Dendroica, www.natureinstruct.org/dendroica
- Xeno-canto, www.xeno-canto.org
- Cornell Lab of Ornithology: Macaulay Library, www.macaulaylibrary.org

Cheat sheets

 THIS LIST IS to be used as a guideline only; it does not cover all the features needed to identify all warblers. It does, however, highlight many important field marks. Before you read this, consider making a chart, key or list like this on your own. By doing it yourself, you will learn and remember the field marks more easily – trust me!

BLACK THROAT

☐ American Redstart ♂ • bright orange patches

☐ Black-throated Blue Warbler ♂ • blue back, black sides

☐ Black-throated Green Warbler ♂ • yellow on sides of head, white wingbars

☐ Golden-winged Warbler ♂ • broad gold wing patch

☐ Black-and-white Warbler ♂ • all black and white

☐ Hooded Warbler ♂ • black hood, yellow face

BLUE OR GRAY THROAT

☐ Connecticut Warbler ♂ • blue hood, eyering

☐ Mourning Warbler ♂ • blue hood, black on chest

☐ Mourning Warbler ♀ • gray hood, no eyering, no black

☐ Golden-winged Warbler ♀ • gray cheek, whitish underneath, gold wing patch

BUFFY THROAT

 ☐ Worm-eating Warbler • head stripes

 ☐ Connecticut Warbler ♀ • eyering

☐ Bay-breasted Warbler ♀ • light chestnut on sides

 ☐ Swainson's Warbler • dull rufous crown, dark eyeline

WHITE OR WHITISH THROAT

Thrush-like

 ☐ Ovenbird • eyering, orange crown stripe

 ☐ Northern Waterthrush • narrow eyebrow, uniform white or buffy underparts

 ☐ Louisiana Waterthrush • flaring eyebrow, white underparts

Distinct Wingbars

 ☐ Chestnut-sided Warbler • chestnut on sides, yellow cap (♀ duller)

☐ Yellow-rumped Warbler • yellow patches on sides and rump (♀ duller)

☐ Blackpoll Warbler ♂ • black cap, black malar stripe

☐ Blackpoll Warbler ♀ • streaked cap, eyeline, pale legs, malar stripe

☐ Black-and-white Warbler ♀ • white eyebrow, white & black back streaks

☐ Cerulean Warbler ♂ • blue head and back, narrow chest band

☐ Cerulean Warbler ♀ • bluish-green above, faint side streaks

No Wingbars

☐ Black-throated Blue Warbler ♀ • small, white wing patch

 ☐ Tennessee Warbler ♂ • grayish head with whitish eyebrow

☐ Tennessee Warbler ♀ • underparts washed with yellow

 ☐ American Redstart ♀ • gray head, yellow patches on sides, tail and wings

Cheat sheets

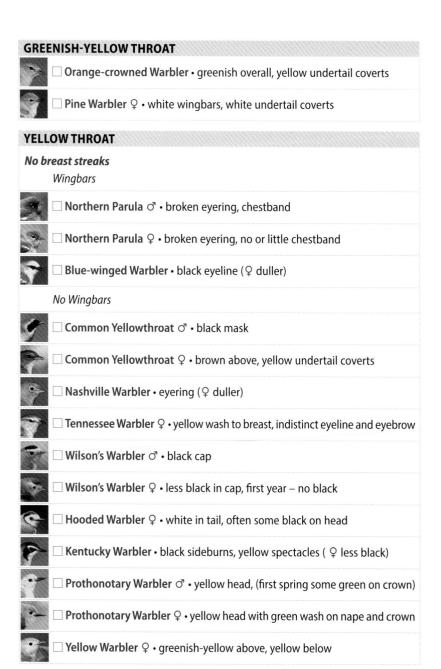

GREENISH-YELLOW THROAT

☐ **Orange-crowned Warbler** • greenish overall, yellow undertail coverts

☐ **Pine Warbler** ♀ • white wingbars, white undertail coverts

YELLOW THROAT

No breast streaks
Wingbars

☐ **Northern Parula** ♂ • broken eyering, chestband

☐ **Northern Parula** ♀ • broken eyering, no or little chestband

☐ **Blue-winged Warbler** • black eyeline (♀ duller)

No Wingbars

☐ **Common Yellowthroat** ♂ • black mask

☐ **Common Yellowthroat** ♀ • brown above, yellow undertail coverts

☐ **Nashville Warbler** • eyering (♀ duller)

☐ **Tennessee Warbler** ♀ • yellow wash to breast, indistinct eyeline and eyebrow

☐ **Wilson's Warbler** ♂ • black cap

☐ **Wilson's Warbler** ♀ • less black in cap, first year – no black

☐ **Hooded Warbler** ♀ • white in tail, often some black on head

☐ **Kentucky Warbler** • black sideburns, yellow spectacles (♀ less black)

☐ **Prothonotary Warbler** ♂ • yellow head, (first spring some green on crown)

☐ **Prothonotary Warbler** ♀ • yellow head with green wash on nape and crown

☐ **Yellow Warbler** ♀ • greenish-yellow above, yellow below

Breast streaks

Distinct Wingbars

• Yellow Rump

 ☐ **Cape May Warbler** ♂ • lots of streaking, chestnut on cheek

☐ **Cape May Warbler** ♀ • duller than male, no chestnut on cheek

 ☐ **Magnolia Warbler** • thick streaks, black cheeks (♀ duller)

• No Yellow Rump

☐ **Pine Warbler** ♂ • light streaking on sides

☐ **Prairie Warbler** ♂ • black eyeline and crescent on cheek

☐ **Prairie Warbler** ♀ • greenish-black eyeline and crescent on cheek

 ☐ **Black-throated Green Warbler** ♀ • yellow on sides of head, black on breast

 ☐ **Blackburnian Warbler** ♀ • yellow (orangish) eyebrow and dark cheeks

 ☐ **Yellow-throated Warbler** • white patch on side of neck, black cheek patch

No or Faint Wingbars

☐ **Palm Warbler** • rusty cap, red streaks, yellow undertail coverts

☐ **Yellow Warbler** ♂ • red streaks on breast (faint streaks on some ♀♀)

☐ **Canada Warbler** • dark necklace, yellow spectacles (♀ duller)

☐ **Kirtland's Warbler** • black lores, broken eyering (♀ duller)

ORANGE THROAT

 ☐ **Blackburnian Warbler** ♂ • orange, black and white

CHESTNUT THROAT

☐ **Bay-breasted Warbler** ♂ • chestnut sides

Author's notes

To Jiffy

For putting up with being a "warbler widow" every May. And for being my best friend.

Special thanks to Lea Martell for making this happen. I would also like to thank Karl Konze, Glenn Barrett, Ron Lohr, and Alan Watson for reviewing earlier drafts. Thanks also go to Rob O. McAleer and Gareth B. Lind for their commitment, creativity and humor throughout the making of this book. Lastly thanks to Julie Takasaki, Stacey Cho, Hartley Millson and George A. Walker for their help on the second edition.

This book would not have been possible without the talent, generosity and patience of the photographers.

– Chris Earley

Photo Credits

Chris G. Earley
Scott Fairbairn
Robert McCaw
John Reaume
Brian E. Small
Judy M Tomlinson
    Photography

Shutterstock:
2009fotofriends
Afonso Farias
Agami Photo Agency
Amanda Guercio
Brian E. Kushner
C. Hamilton
Christopher Unsworth
FotoRequest
Jay Ondreicka
Jukka Jantunen
Martin Pelanek
Matthew Jolley

Melinda Fawver
M. Leonard Photography
Nick Pecker
Paul Reeves Photography
Paul Sparks
punkbirdr
Ray Hennessy
Sage Sienna
Stubble Field Photography
vagabond54
Wilfred Marissen
Wingman Photography

Index

SHUTTERSTOCK/RAY HENNESSY

Louisiana Waterthrush • pages 20–21

REAUME

Louisiana Waterthrush • pages 20–21

REAUME

Northern Waterthrush • pages 22–23

SHUTTERSTOCK/MATTHEW JOLLEY

Northern Waterthrush • pages 22–23

	Eyebrow color	Eyebrow shape	Beak	Throat	Color of underpants	Streaking of underpants	Leg color	Tail movement	Song
Northern	Uniformly light yellow, may be buffy or whitish	Usually gets thinner behind eye	Thinner and shorter	Often dark spots on throat	Usually light yellow, buffy or whitish throughout	Usually arranged in defined lines	Usually dull pink	Bobs its tail up and down	A loud series of fluid notes *weet weet weet weet wee wee wee chew chew chew*
Louisiana	Bright white but slightly grayish or buffy in front of eye	Broader and stays the same thickness	Thicker and longer	Usually no spots on throat	Often cinnamon buff on flanks contrasting with white underpants	Usually more spread out and blurrier	Usually very bright pink	Bobs entire rear half of its body up and down with some sideways movement	Starts off with a few loud whistles, then changes to a scrambled mix of quieter twittering notes

Fall Comparison 1

Photos with a * show spring plumage that is similar to fall plumage.

Black-throated Blue* • pages 86–87

SHUTTERSTOCK/ AGAMI PHOTO AGENCY

Tennessee • pages 36–37

FAIRBAIRN

Orange-crowned • pages 38–39

SHUTTERSTOCK/ WINGMAN PHOTOGRAPHY

Wilson's • pages 104–105

EARLEY

Yellow • pages 78–79

SMALL

ooded* • pages 52–53

SHUTTERSTOCK/ AGAMI PHOTO AGENCY

rothonotary* • pages 32–33

REAUME

	Eyebrow	Eyeline	Eyering	Wings	Undertail coverts	Tail length in relation to body size	Tail spots	Legs
Prothonotary – fall female	None	None	None	Plain bluish-gray	White	Short	Large white	Dark
Hooded – first fall female	Yellow	Dusky lore	None	Plain olive-green	Yellow	Long	Large white	Pinkish or brownish
Wilson's – first fall female	Yellow	None	None	Plain olive-green	Yellow	Long	None	Pinkish or brownish
Yellow – first fall female	None	None	None or yellowish	Feathers edged with yellow	Yellow	Short to average	Yellow	Pinkish or brownish
Orange-crowned (look for faint streaks on sides of breast)	Short and indistinct whitish (or yellowish)	Short and indistinct, dusky	Broken, thin, (whitish or yellowish)	Plain dull olive	Yellowish	Long	None	Dark
Tennessee – first fall	Long, yellowish	Long and dusky	None	Plain olive-green	White (or tinged with pale yellow)	Short	Usually none or very small	Dark
Black-throated Blue – first fall female	Long, whitish or buffy	None	An arc under eye	Plain olive brown (maybe hint of blue)	Buffy	Average	Usually none or very light	Dark to pale brown

Bay-breasted • pages 74–75

SHUTTERSTOCK/
MARTIN PELANEK

Chestnut-sided • pages 80–83

SHUTTERSTOCK/

Blackpoll • pages 84–85

SHUTTERSTOCK/
PAUL REEVES PHOTOGRAPHY

Pine* • pages 90–91

SMALL

first-year female • pages 90–91

REAUME

Fall Comparison 2

Photos with a * show spring plumage
that is similar to fall plumage.

	Undertail coverts	Head pattern	Breast color	Back streaking	Tail length in relation to body size	Wing feathers	Sides	Legs
Pine	White or light brownish buff	Usually shows a darkish cheek patch, faint eyeline and a light arc under the eye	Yellow or brownish	None	Long	Edged brownish – primaries not tipped with white	Olive or brownish	Dark
Blackpoll	Usually white but may have pale yellow	Usually has a distinct dark eyeline and pale eyebrow	Usually bright greenish yellow	Faintly or strongly streaked	Short	Edged with white – primaries tipped with white	Some olive on flanks	May be dark or light
Bay-breasted	Usually buff	Usually has a very indistinct eyeline and eyebrow	Usually a dull or buffy yellow	Faintly or strongly streaked	Short	Edged with white – primaries tipped with white	Some show distinct or indistinct chestnut on flanks	Dark
Chestnut-sided	White	Gray face with white eyering	White or grayish	Faintly or strongly streaked	Long	Edged yellowish	Some show distinct or indistinct chestnut on flanks	Dark

Fall Comparison 3

Photos with a * show spring plumage that is similar to fall plumage.

Orange-crowned* • pages 38–39 SMALL

Common Yellowthroat • pages 50–51 SHUTTERSTOCK/ CHRISTOPHER UNSWORTH

Tennessee • pages 36–37 FAIRBAIRN

Connecticut • pages 44–45 TOMLINSON

Nashville* • pages 40–43 SMALL

Northern Parula • pages 66–69 SHUTTERSTOCK/ AGAMI PHOTO AGENCY

Canada* • pages 102–103 FAIRBAIRN

Magnolia • pages 70–73 SHUTTERSTOCK/ PAUL REEVES PHOTOGRAPHY

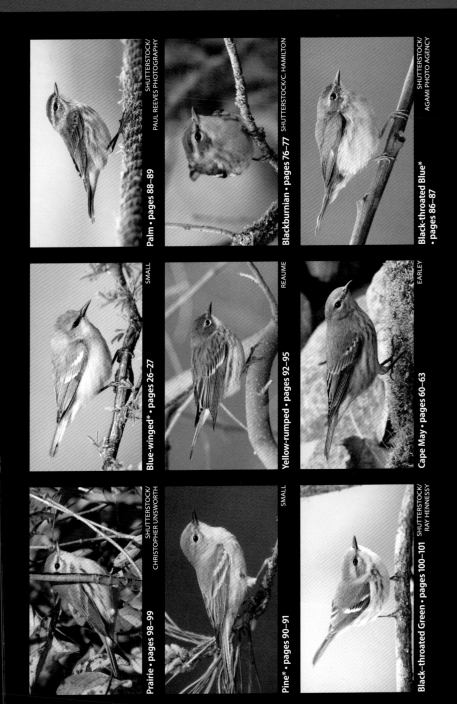

Palm • pages 88–89
SHUTTERSTOCK/ PAUL REEVES PHOTOGRAPHY

Blackburnian • pages 76–77 SHUTTERSTOCK/C. HAMILTON

Black-throated Blue* • pages 86–87
SHUTTERSTOCK/ AGAMI PHOTO AGENCY

Blue-winged* • pages 26–27 SMALL

Yellow-rumped • pages 92–95 REAUME

Cape May • pages 60–63 EARLEY

Prairie • pages 98–99
SHUTTERSTOCK/ CHRISTOPHER UNSWORTH

Pine* • pages 90–91 SMALL

Black-throated Green • pages 100–101
SHUTTERSTOCK/ RAY HENNESSY

Spring Comparison

Spring Comparison
Adult Males
continued on back panel

SMALL — Connecticut • pages 44–45

SMALL — Nashville • pages 40–43

REAUME — Mourning • pages 46–47

SMALL — Orange-crowned • pages 38–39

McCAW — Common Yellowthroat • pages 50–51